FROM THE LION ROCK

Described in *The Listener* as 'a demanding, elliptical drama, beauti-
fully written, and convincingly recreating an exotic world—the world
of Kubla Khan and the old books of travel and oriental romance,'
From The Lion Rock takes us to Sri Lanka in the fifth century A.D.,
and to an earthly paradise on a mountaintop: Sigiriya, at once fortress
and palace, built by a king who killed his father to gain the throne.
The palace crowns a gigantic outcrop rising from a level plain and
moulded into the form of a lion, facing India—where the tyrant's
brother has fled to gather an avenging army. The tale of the Lion
King and his fate is told by the seer and astrologer Hormazdyar,
called from his village to become adviser to the Lion Throne. Will
the king, secure as a god on the heights of Sigiriya, survive the
coming invasion? Tell the truth and be executed for it, or equivo-
cate and live: this is the choice facing Hormazdyar. 'The brilliant,
complex imagery of Carey Harrison's dramatic "poems",' wrote *The
Times*, 'is heard at its characteristic best in *From The Lion Rock*.'

THE SEA VOYAGE

Called 'a triumph' by *The Times* and 'a veritable feast for the ears'
by *The Listener*, these three plays tell the story of the Fourth Armada
of the Isles of Spice, a circumnavigation of the globe launched from
Seville in 1527, in search of a prize greater than gold or spice; greater
than territorial conquest; greater than any treasure dreamt of by a
Christian King. Their mission is to find a holy relic, buried 'like old
Adam, to the east of paradise': relic of relics: the Bones of Christ.
'We have journeyed,' wrote *The Listener*, 'deep into some very strange
territory, where the magical and the mystical rub shoulders with the
sordid and the crude, purple passages of lyrical description give way
to scenes of earthy farce, and an utterly alien world, rich in exotic
detail, is forever opening up around us.'

FROM THE LION ROCK
& the SEA VOYAGE trilogy

plays for radio

Carey Harrison

THE OLEANDER PRESS

The Oleander Press Limited
17 Stansgate Avenue
Cambridge CB2 2QZ
England

The Oleander Press
210 Fifth Avenue
New York, N.Y. 10010
U.S.A.

ISBN 0-906672-61-9

British Library Cataloguing in Publication Data
Harrison, Carey
From the Lion Rock: and the Sea Voyage
  trilogy: plays for radio
I. Title II. Harrison, Carey: Sea Voyage
822.914

ISBN 0-906672-61-9

13/1000

Printed and bound in Great Britain

Contents

✺

✺

FROM THE LION ROCK

For Seneka

For Sam and for Penelope, with thanks,
and Bill and Verla,
for the journey to Sigiriya

Preface

Sigiriya, the Lion Rock, lies at the heart of Sri Lanka both geographi-
cally and historically. Fourteen centuries ago its royal palace was
built by the usurper of a Buddhist kingdom; and was destroyed
within a generation. Then as now, Buddhism was no antidote to
civil strife. An El Dorado swallowed by the jungle like the temples
of Angkor Wat, the Lion Rock lay forgotten until a 19th century
hunting party came upon it by chance. Today the rock can be
climbed by the visitor — the stout-hearted visitor, I should say, since
the ascent is as perilous as ever — to explore what remains of the
palace, one of the archaeological wonders of the world. I have taken
liberties with the history of the Lion Rock and, of necessity, invented
characters and ceremonies; altered names. Some of the more exotic
names can prove a stumbling block to reading (let alone to actors
charged with saying them aloud), so a brief guide may be helpful,
authoritative only insofar as it conveys the way I heard them in my
head: Hormazdyar the Persian — though a secondary stress should be
given to the final syllable; Fa Hsien the traveller is Fa *Shen*; King
Virabahu; Kalyanavati the courtesan; Lokesvara, warden of the
caskets; Anandaraja, 'love's commissioner'. Of the places: Hormazdyar's village of Hundaravapi; and most vexing of all, the Royal City,
Anuradhapura, the stress so vigorous in this instance (it was and is
a real place) that the subsequent 'a' almost vanishes altogether in
the tumble of the last three syllables. And while wrestling with
these, imagine in the background — if you will — the greater cacophony of the jungle, chattering in a thousand tongues, and crying
out for decipherment. This is our hero's trade: Hormazdyar is a seer,
a village wise man tempted, in his old age, to see the world from the
tyrant's vantage point, a palace in the sky — the Lion Rock.

From The Lion Rock, commissioned by the BBC World Service, was first broadcast by them on March 19, 1988, and subsequently on BBC Radio 3 on September 5, 1989. The cast was as follows:

HORMAZDYAR	Joss Ackland
FA HSIEN	Sam Dastor
VIRABAHU	John Shrapnel
KALYANAVATI	Karen Archer
SUBHA	David March
TISSA	Stephen Rashbrook
OX-CART DRIVER	John Hollis
ANULA	Mary Wimbush
BLIND GIRL	Annabelle Lanyon

Director: Gordon House

Crows, distant, mocking.

A moment's pause. Then peacock screams, nearer. The peacock screams continue, intermittent, then fade to silence.

A sound of bees, close.

HORMAZDYAR. Bees. In the rising heat of day, the poet says, a bee prises open a tight red bud and crawls into the dark sanctuary.

Gradually, as the voice resumes, the bees fade to silence.

Waking, just before waking, I see in my mind's eye a place that might be mine to cherish one day, when I grow to manhood. The confluence of two rivers. I am gazing from the heron's wing; no, from the eagle's wing, hovering, still, I am dawn itself. Sandbank and jungle and outcrop of rock black as the moon, and two slow green rivers joining forces. A place that might be mine to love one day, when I am old.

Bee sound has gone. The crows return distantly, now taking off, as they squawk, in a great flapping of wings.

And then at once, waking, waking but with the landscape before me in my mind's eye, I remember that I am old, that I have grown to manhood, that there is no room in my heart (no room except for an instant this morning just before waking) for a landscape to cherish, for a place to be mine: all the places I've known have grown transparent, just by looking at them. Looking through them, if you will, through the veil of appearances. The veil of maya: too much looking and you rub it threadbare. *(A beat)* But I am Hormazdyar the seer, the stargazer, it is my task to pierce the veil, people expect it of me. Well, then: pierce the veil. To see . . . what? A darkness. You could call it that. Like dreams, the stars themselves darken —

Urgent whispers interrupt him, overlapping each other:

FA HSIEN. You can tell me the truth. Shall I return safe to Kwangchow?

TISSA. The girl Mitta, master. Is she the one?

SUBHA. Lokesvara, warden of the caskets, seeks my office, by slander. I must know what—

TISSA. Is she the one for me? Master?

A beat.

VIRABAHU. Speak, Persian. Is the day propitious for battle—or for parasols?

KALYANAVATI. That rose in my bed, master. *(She laughs)* Tell me. Was it from you?

HORMAZDYAR *(close)*. Like dreams, the stars darken . . .

VIRABAHU. Don't you *know* the hour of your death, astrologer?

HORMAZDYAR *(to him)*. No, not the hour. Among the stars death has no meaning.

Virabahu grunts, amused. His chuckle fading.

Only danger, conflict, and delight: these are pre-ordained. The several paths a man may take, but not what he will meet there. In the heavens as on earth there are countless particulars whose confluence we call chance, infinite contradictions in the play of starlight, enough to deflect the gravest danger, at the last. Like dreams, the stars darken by day. and dawn brings the blessing of Ormazd the creator, lord of light: the blessing of uncertainty.

A moment.

By his grace, then, I could only see the outlines. Never the outcome.

A single, drawn-out peacock cry.

Until I came to the Lion Rock.

Footsteps: slippers, padding lightly down a corridor, in a slight echo acoustic.

VIRABAHU *(no echo)*. If not the hour, don't you know the manner of your death, Persian?

Jingling bells added to the footsteps, approaching. Both come to a halt.

KALYANAVATI *(faint echo)*. I am Kalyanavati, master, consort of the fifth rank.

Brief swish of silk, tinkle of bells as she bows. This and her words in the echo acoustic. Hormazdyar, close (as before), no echo:

HORMAZDYAR. Kalyanavati. Garlanded with shells, girdled with little tinkling bells. Her eyes like water lilies. I followed her into a corridor of mirrors, ascending the rock.

KALYANAVATI. Come, master! Don't let the mirrors distract you. Keep your gaze fixed on me. Come!

HORMAZDYAR. Like her reflections chasing her in vain, I followed. Once in Anuradhapura, in my youth, I wore silk slippers, trod marble, and studied for a year under the Court Astrologer, Lord Kitta. I was glad, even then, to return home. Glad of obscurity. For twenty years I journeyed no further than a yoking of oxen, a day's march, from my village. But the Lion King has eyes everywhere.

The creak — intermittent — of an ox-cart with one squeaky wheel.

When Kitta died I was sent for. *(Amused)* Councillor Subha, lord of Elevation and Disgrace, promised me a chariot drawn by Sindhu-steeds, to bring me to King Virabahu, Prince of the Wise. Instead it was an ox-cart with a creaking wheel.

Behind the creaking cart, crows, distant.

South of the Royal City I met Fa Hsien the traveller, a devout straightforward fellow from the land of Han, in China. He too was making his way to the Lion Throne.

FA HSIEN *(hesitant; half a question:)*. Then — you are one of those who know.

HORMAZDYAR. A credulous fellow. Yet anxious not to seem a fool. *(To him)* Know *what*?

FA HSIEN. All things. Our past and future — mine, this driver's here, even the King's. Our karma.

DRIVER. *What's* he know?

FA HSIEN. Your fate, man. He reads it in the stars.

DRIVER. I piss on his stars.

The cart creaks.

My fate. (*He gives a snort*) My fate is to drive a cart with one complaining wheel. It's a fault in the wood.

HORMAZDYAR. You've tried goose fat?

DRIVER. Of *course* I've tried goose fat. It still creaks: it's a fault in the wood. Listen.

A moment as they listen to the creaking.

FA HSIEN. In Anuradhapura a merchant offered me red silk, 'silk from Cathay!', and my eyes filled with tears. I beg you . . . can you tell me if I'll see Kwangchow again?

DRIVER. *He* can't tell you. *He* doesn't know if we'll make it to the top of this hill.

Above the toiling ox-cart, migrating swans call out in flight.

HORMAZDYAR. You whose eyes are better than mine: above us there — what birds are those?

FA HSIEN. Geese, surely.

DRIVER. Swans.

FA HSIEN (*excited*). *Tibetan* geese!

DRIVER. Are you *both* blind? They're swans. Would geese be flying north? They winter here.

HORMAZDYAR. Like you, Fa Hsien. (*A beat*) Swans flying north-ward: a good omen for your return.

FA HSIEN. But —

HORMAZDYAR. Trust it.

FA HSIEN (*tentative*). You *know*, then?

The whispers return, overlapping, vexed:

SUBHA. The King wishes to know many things, astrologer. You understand, I hope.

KALYANAVATI. *Why* won't you tell me, master? Am I not important enough?

TISSA. All I want's a simple answer: yes or no.

KALYANAVATI. Is that why? Master?

TISSA. Must I pay you more?

VIRABAHU. I was informed that you were wise in divination, but slow to prophesy. Tongue-tied, even. *(Fading)* I *know you*, Persian.

A loud creak from the cart.

HORMAZDYAR. I know this much, Fa Hsien: you'll shed more tears when we reach our destination.

FA HSIEN *(wary)*. Ah? Why?

HORMAZDYAR. Because flowers from your country bloom there, so I'm told. Flowers of great beauty. Roses.

DRIVER. Flowers? Wait till you see the girls.

A moment.

FA HSIEN. Is it true that the rock itself is painted — *(he hesitates)* — with faces . . .

DRIVER. Faces. Bodies. Female bodies. Breasts — some of them as big as this cartwheel. Bigger. You're not the first to cross deserts to see them.

A beat.

King Virabahu has a private walkway that circles the rock, hidden behind a wall. Inside, the wall is lacquered like a mirror. So as he walks, he's got . . . bodies on either side. And him reflected, in between.

FA HSIEN. Yet he himself . . . is he not a pious man? The Lion King owns many precious relics, surely. A lock of the Buddha's hair? His rinsing bowl, of silver?

DRIVER. I shouldn't wonder. Look hard enough, you'll probably find the Buddha's pisspot, too.

He chuckles.

If that's what you've come to see.

The creaking fades, ceases.

HORMAZDYAR. Picture a crouching lion hundreds of feet high. Picture a rock reaching to the clouds, rising like an axe-head at the centre of a level plain ringed by mountains. With a palace at its summit. And the rock moulded in brick and plaster, paws at its base, jaws and eyes and a mane above: the Lion Rock. We halted at the edge of the great plain, still a full day's ride away, and gazed at it.

DRIVER. Some evenings when you look up you can see the court sitting there like statues in heaven. The Damask Pavilion, that's where they sit, on gold. And the king never moves, he just gazes out over our heads, across the sea, to India and beyond, they say, to the edge of the world.

Wind rising sharply. Closer, a tinkling of bells.

KALYANAVATI. Don't be afraid. Look: from here you can see the pleasure gardens.

HORMAZDYAR. Far below us, lakes fountains playing, trees, parasols. Triumphal arches, pennons, flowers, embroidered canopies and banners. Parasols winking blue and white like water lilies, at the edge of ornamental lakes: all ordered, all foreseen, foreknown. A human void erasing, as far as the eye can see, the hand of meaning, as water spilling on the page disperses brush strokes. Yet another page effaced. Human; transparent now; the mirror of our eyes.

Crows, distant.

In my yard, a beggar kneels. Puts down his alms bowl, brings out—ah: not a beggar. A petitioner; a client. He brings out two short strips of bamboo, cut lengthwise, and places them against his forehead. Thinks, concentrates: before throwing them down. If both fall on their flat surface he will not consult me. If on their curved surface, he must change the question. If one on each, half and half, the moment is auspicious. Now—which will it be?—he throws—

KALYANAVATI. *This* way, master! Only the king enters the palace through the lion's jaws.

Wind continuing, gusting sharply.

Take my hand. Together we must dare the heights.

Footsteps, cautious, as they climb. Now and then a soft sound of bells.

HORMAZDYAR. Her eyes like water lilies.

KALYANAVATI. Your skin is as fair as mine. Where do you come from?

HORMAZDYAR. From the Kumbasi-district. The village of Hundara-vapi.

KALYANAVATI. They say you are a Roman.

HORMAZDYAR. Do they?

KALYANAVATI. Yes.

Whispers:

SUBHA. They say . . .

TISSA. They say . . .

FA HSIEN. They say a compound of . . .

SUBHA. A walnut freshly shelled, after a three days' fast . . .

VIRABAHU. They say you know the potion of immortality.

FA HSIEN. Brain-shaped, like the scarab . . .

SUBHA. A compound of . . .

KALYANAVATI (*loud, alarmed*). Careful, master!

Loud: a sound of bees.

Master! Take care! My hand, quick—or you'll fall!

Bees fading in a gust of wind.

HORMAZDYAR. Falling, ravished by air.

Wind, and a flapping sound: crows rising, cawing distantly.

SUBHA. Hormazdyar of Hundaravapi, in the Kumbasi-district?

HORMAZDYAR (*puzzled*). Yes?

A moment.

SUBHA. You live modestly, if I may say so. Is this your house?

HORMAZDYAR. This is my house, yes. I was born here.

Both voices in an indoor acoustic.

SUBHA. I am his Majesty's councillor Subha, lord of Elevation and Disgrace.

HORMAZDYAR. Anula, fetch some wine.

Soft footsteps, departing. A moment.

SUBHA. As you may be aware, the lord Kitta, lately astrologer to the Lion Throne, thought little of your talents as a student. (*A beat*) Was he a hard taskmaster?

HORMAZDYAR. Forgive me: *lately* astrologer?

SUBHA. He has been dead nine months. You didn't know?

Soft footsteps returning. A moment.

Yes, the lord Kitta was disappointed in you. He would not have recommended you. (*A beat*) But then—the King was disappointed in the lord Kitta . . .

A moment. Wine being poured.

Thank you. And *your* fame has spread.

Wine pours into a second glass.

HORMAZDYAR. Thank you, Anula.

SUBHA. Until we could find no-one worthier than you to fill the office.

There were other candidates, of course, but when — *(he breaks off)* — why do you smile?

HORMAZDYAR. Court Astrologer? Why on earth would I want to be Court Astrologer, at my age?

A drawn-out peacock scream, and then a brief tinkling of bells, closer.

KALYANAVATI. Slowly, master. Lean on me. This is the room called Shadow-covered. It is yours.

A moment.

HORMAZDYAR *(to us)*. Red drapes; damascened silk; red silk from Cathay.

KALYANAVATI. You feel better?

HORMAZDYAR *(faintly, to her)*. Better, yes. The height made me dizzy. I heard bees. Or did I dream them?

KALYANAVATI. No: they protect the Lion Rock. *(Amused)* Especially against Romans. *(Bells jingling as she moves)* Here is your rinsing bowl, and ladle. Fresh clothes. Feel them. It was a long climb, I know. Shall I pour you some sugar-water?

HORMAZDYAR. Thank you, no.

KALYANAVATI. Or some wine? If you still feel faint, I could rub your feet with oil of sweet basil. Here is your bed. *(A moment)* Master?

HORMAZDYAR. Rest; a bed; a weary bee, I pried apart the tight red bud and crawled into the dark sanctuary. *(A beat)* Beside my bed I dreamt a white-eared dragon; with its breath it lit the candles in my room. Waking I saw it was Kalyanavati. But I was not awake. The white-eared dragon rose and bit her girdle in two; as the garments fell, the earth gaped and she sank alive into a great watery tank that steamed and splashed and stank of wine . . .

Kalyanavati laughing quietly, as if Hormazdyar had told her the dream.

HORMAZDYAR. At last I slept.

Indoor acoustic gives way to the sound of crickets.

Night thoughts. Sometimes I feel tempted to commit them to paper, in the old Persian script, in my father's slow hand. But here in Hundaravapi even my own boy cannot read it, so why bother?

Humming, close (Hormazdyar humming). Distantly, a heron-cry. Close, the sound of writing.

Candlelight. A sigh, bird cries, a scent of faded jasmine, a shutter rattles as a bat brushes the blind. Or is it the wind? Out in the yard a group of scattered pebbles awaits me in the moonlight, a broken bamboo shoot split three ways. In troubled times each glance turns into divination. Herons in flight against the moon: how many? The will of the gods is everywhere and nowhere. Withheld from us; surrounding us; hidden openly. I hear myself humming. What tune? What words?

The sound of writing fades. Sound of crickets, continuing.

But outside my window: no yard. Instead, the precipice. Last night a palace guard fell to his death from his narrow ledge on the face of the rock. They are devised, these ledges, so that if a watchman falls asleep . . . he will awake, if ever, falling.

A moment.

Sometimes I walk the parapet to cure my fear of heights. Above, the night sky bright with stars like a scattering of seed. I feel the sky inside me. Dawn coming, the promise of reason, and my veins, my blood, respond; just as flowers open, in answer to the light: earthbound stars. Adjacency, affinity, proportion, sympathy: all things compare, and man, god's echo, is the fulcrum.

A beat.

Her eyes — her eyes like water lilies. Such is the world, unending emulation and analogy. To the rat is it a rat-universe, whiskered and clawed, a world that slithers and pounces and gorges itself? Will no-one tell me why it is to man alone that the key is given, the key to the Great Harmony of things? The walnut, brain-shaped, heals the brain. But does the rat know this? Without man, would God despair, his song mere sound? Beyond the pleasure gardens, beyond the lakes, walls, dykes, and ramparts, looms the dull mass of the jungle, feathery grey with fog.

A brief, tentative peacock cry. Closer, the sound of writing resumes.

Out there, the world crying expound! explain! In the wilderness, in the sacred space where understanding fails, magic and poetry come face to face, and divination is all. Here, on this painted rock, voided by artifice, there is too much light. Emerging from the mist, the sun rises behind Dawn Mountain, and for a moment the inverted lotus of the temple glistens white: a monastery called Invisible Dragon.

A moment, then the peacocks begin to cry, a rising chorus drowning the sound of writing. As they fade:

SUBHA. Hormazdyar of Hundaravapi: follow me. You are to attend the dawn audience.

As the cries cease, slow drums begin.

FA HSIEN. I, Fa Hsien the traveller, that have crossed the Gobi on foot, the Hindu Kush, and the length of India, came to the Lion Rock and witnessed these things: five hundred feet above the jungle, a palace playing with fountains and music, where men gathered like clouds to see the God-king in his glory.

Blowing of conches, as the drums continue.

At daybreak, we entered the sandalwood pavilion, led by attendants in procession, holding aloft the parasol, the yak-tail whisk, the jewelled fan, the shell with water, and the sword. The fan was ivory, the parasol white with a coral foot and silver shank.

Behind Fa Hsien, distantly, a voice proclaiming:

SUBHA. Virabahu, the World-Honoured, the Conqueror, Founder of the Lion Throne, descendant of the Sun, called Maurya, Peacock, Immortal, Architect and Father of the Kingdom.

The distant proclamation ends in a clash of cymbals and a great fluttering of wings.

Drums continuing.

FA HSIEN. At the rear of the pavilion a door opened and doves flew out over our heads to circle the rock, while in their wake, hidden at first by the unfolding wings, white-robed, came the King.

A single blast of the conch, and silence.

No drums. The wind is audible, beating at the rock.

No sooner had he settled on the Lion Throne than one by one, in order of precedence, courtiers approached, knelt and received the gift of bread — for beside the throne, at one arm, were heaped sweet cakes, the mound they formed resembling the rock itself. At the other arm, a heap of skulls; like so many gourds. Those in disfavour, it is said, look up to find — instead of bread — a skull at their fingertips, and in this manner learn of their doom. The King spoke to none that day except the magus Hormazdyar, whom I had met on my travels and knew by sight.

Subha's voice, and those of Virabahu and Hormazdyar, above the wind:

SUBHA. Hormazdyar of Hundaravapi, step forward.

VIRABAHU. You are Hormazdyar?

HORMAZDYAR. I am.

VIRABAHU. You are younger than Kitta your predecessor. And yet older than I expected. Come closer. Are you as old in wisdom as they say?

HORMAZDYAR. Older than I was before I climbed this rock, great king. I thought each step would be my last.

VIRABAHU. But you knew it would not be.

A moment.

Well?

HORMAZDYAR. I was mortally afraid.

VIRABAHU. Mortally? *(A beat)* Mortally. Don't you *know* the hour of your death, astrologer?

HORMAZDYAR. Ptolemy writes: even when there is danger, the

argument is never finished.

VIRABAHU. Do the stars argue over a man's death?

HORMAZDYAR. Unceasingly. Among the stars death has no meaning.

VIRABAHU. Among men death has a way of closing the argument, as you may have noticed. Surely there is an hour for everyone. Appointed in the stars.

HORMAZDYAR. Perhaps. But to identify it —

VIRABAHU. Is your task. *(A beat)* Harder in some cases, no doubt. Did you hear me proclaimed immortal?

HORMAZDYAR. Yes.

VIRABAHU. And am I?

A pause. Amused:

You may speak plainly.

A moment.

It's a riddle, astrologer. Shall I tell you the answer? Look around. Where are we?

HORMAZDYAR. On the Lion Rock.

VIRABAHU. Where else?

HORMAZDYAR. Between heaven and earth.

VIRABAHU. Yes: where the hours are without number. So . . . who can tell how long a man may live, between heaven and earth? *(A beat)* Unless he falls.

A moment, the wind audible.

Below us lies the world's reckoning: what do you see there?

HORMAZDYAR. Your pleasure gardens.

VIRABAHU. Look inward. Can you see the armies of India, their banners and war elephants? I can. The disposition of their forces? Can you foresee the day of their defeat?

A pause.

In time you will. The stars will assist you.

HORMAZDYAR. I serve *them*. I am neither seer nor prophet.

VIRABAHU. You deal in prophecy.

HORMAZDYAR. Is divination prophecy?

VIRABAHU. Persian: for mincing words I had your predecessor put to death. I say you deal in prophecy. What else do you learn from gazing at the stars?

HORMAZDYAR. Patience. If we seek more, they blind us.

VIRABAHU. Are you afraid to look, then — as you were afraid to climb? *(A beat)* Well?

HORMAZDYAR. Climbing the rock I was afraid to look down. Not to look up. The contest above mirrors our own; and sometimes, as on earth, the weakest triumphs: I reached the summit. *(A moment)* The heavens teach us what we may not know, however hard we look.

VIRABAHU. What we may not know?

HORMAZDYAR. I say again: there is a contest above, as there is below: the contest inside us: that and that alone is mirrored in the stars.

VIRABAHU. And the future?

HORMAZDYAR. Many futures: the several paths a man may take, but not what he will meet there.

VIRABAHU. Persian —

HORMAZDYAR. *That* will be contested to the last. By one gleam of distant Aldebaran — so says Basilides — may stand or fall the equipoise of Jupiter and Saturn.

VIRABAHU. Never mind Basilides. Speak to me of the future.

HORMAZDYAR. As fortune tellers do? *(Mimicking)* Great King, immortal, your seed will live for ever. When Saturn is in the Scorpion's house you will scatter your enemies. *(A beat)* So it is foretold, is it not? In every market-place.

A moment.

VIRABAHU. Who brought this stick of insolence to me? This Persian crow?

A silence. Wind, loud. Above it:

Send him back to the Kumbasi-district. In irons.

A peacock cry, roused by the King's voice.

VIRABAHU. Better, hold him in irons here and starve him till he prophesies.

Crows rising, mocking. When their cawing fades, the wind has gone, leaving a sound of crickets in their place. Outdoor acoustic:

ANULA. Foolish old man: d'you think you'll see more of the world from a palace? A demon has possessed you — placed an elephant-goad on your head and driven you mad.

HORMAZDYAR. Anula . . .

With a loud creak, the ox-cart with the squeaking wheel gets under way.

ANULA. Look around. This is your village.

HORMAZDYAR. Anula, let go.

ANULA. You are honoured here.

HORMAZDYAR *(close; to us:)*. Honoured. Loved, fed. Content.

ANULA *(distantly now)*. Hormazdyar!

The creaking continues, fades very gradually as Hormazdyar speaks.

HORMAZDYAR. For twenty years I had hidden from it, and now it was as if the sun had found me out, in the deepest of thickets. Even with my eyes shut it drew me. But what was it that drew me? Not curiosity. Fate? I believed then that there was no such thing: a winding path, a thousand crossroads and at each a choice. Or rather that it *was* written; but must not be read. Only prepared for: this was the wise man's task, and the wise man's advice. One gleam of distant

Aldebaran . . . enough to reveal our destiny, to the impatient and the unready always too late: so I thought. In my youth there were seven kingdoms, fated — you might say — to be unified under the peacemaker, King Sena. Virabahu's father. Now the world had a centre and all paths led to it like spokes. This world: who was more *of* it than I, reading the shape of every cloud, counting the bird cries, numbering the moonlit pebbles in my yard? And still I could not say what drew me.

Distantly, the sound of a flute.

Until, by chance it seemed, making slowly for the Lion Rock, we stopped for water in the rising heat of day, on the road to Anuradhapura.

GIRL (*eager*). Who's there? Who are you?

HORMAZDYAR. A man came out to us from a house hidden by trees, a young full-grown fellow, bearded, with a girl of ten beside him. Before I knew it she had run to me, flung herself tight against my arm, seizing my hand in hers, and at once, with the fingers of her free hand, begun to play on my palm as if her fingers were talking, as if they were searching my face for its shape, or my mind for words, and I realized she was blind.

GIRL. This way, master. Follow me.

HORMAZDYAR. Fingers plucking at my palm as at an instrument.

GIRL. This is my garden, Fire Domain. I planted it; my father tends it with me. And this is the bridge called Force-of-arms. Can you guess its story?

HORMAZDYAR. The stream had water-lilies in it, blue as dragonflies, and frogs that watched the waterflies like sated potentates. She led me across a bridge of broad uneven planks, into a grove. I knew its name before she told me. And I knew this blind child's future, saw beyond her fair thin eager face as if I too were blind and saw within, saw her wedding and her joy, her children, and the griefs that children bring. Saw; in the darkness of the grove.

GIRL. Stay close. It's darker still for me, master. But I know the way.

HORMAZDYAR. At the centre of it stood a bo-tree. Looking round, looking closer now, I saw that all the other trees were only branches grown into the earth to re-emerge.

GIRL. My father says this place was named for me. But it was here before we came, and named for everyone who visits it. This is the grove called Sight Regained. From here you can see Fire Domain, and Arrow Fountain where the stream rises. Shall I fetch you some water?

HORMAZDYAR. And she led me out of the grove, never once letting go of my hand, across the broad-planked bridge, towards the house; the house still hidden, where a flute played. (*A beat*) Sometimes I think she is still with me, I feel her fingers scurry like spiders across my open palm. And when I feel them the future comes to me like an old thing half-remembered, like a dream before it fades. The gift of second sight is mine now, as though it had always been there — only the spiders in my palm to tell it from a simple act of memory. But if I speak, will the gift remain?

Wind rising, drowning the flute. Crows, distantly, fading slowly.

That same day, meeting Fa Hsien outside the Royal City, on the road to the Lion Rock, I felt her fingers tell me his story, saw him shipwrecked, wandering footsore, returning to Canton, storm-tossed but safe. And when I met the Great King I felt again the pricking at my palm, and knew it all, his life, his death and mine. Remembered it, and could not speak.

Wind fades. Close, bells jingle.

Not for us, to speak with the creator's voice. My reward: to lie manacled in the room called Shadow-covered while Kalyanavati came and went with sugar-water, bowls of scented petals, balm to soothe my ankles where the irons chafed.

The bells have faded, departing. Barely a pause.

The lord Subha was also most attentive.

SUBHA. If you need entrails, Persian, they can be provided. Animal or human. Fresh, should you require it. Or decayed? Is there an art in counting maggots?

HORMAZDYAR. Everything can be expounded. Even maggots.

SUBHA. Well then —

HORMAZDYAR (*interrupting*). Never underestimate the maggot.

SUBHA. I beg your pardon?

HORMAZDYAR (*a touch of delirium*). From a maggot is born the phoenix, lord of jubilees, that lives twelve thousand years and more. So says Roman Pliny.

SUBHA. Indeed? (*A beat*) You know much, Hormazdyar. Is it so hard to find the words to satisfy a king?

A moment.

HORMAZDYAR (*calm; to us*). As the rains came scorpions visited me too, and spiders, clawed like crabs. I dreamt: dreamt of the herons wheeling in the winter skies over Hundaravapi. Orange puddles out of magenta soil. Earthly horoscopes crying expound! explain! Rice stems strung with crystal, shivering in the breeze —

Tinkling of bells, fainter, departing —

Was it her beside me, or only her fragrance in the air?

KALYANAVATI. Master —

HORMAZDYAR (*to her; in the starvation-delirium*). According to Herodotus of Halicarnassus, the Egyptian priests believe that each of us has his twin, whom it is ominous to meet —

KALYANAVATI. Have you seen how thin you are, how near to death? Look.

HORMAZDYAR (*to us*). And in the jewelled mirror I saw: Hormazdyar haruspex, he who squints into the future like a carnival beggar, for the price of a garland of shells, or an embroidered handkerchief. Or a bowl of rice. (*A moment*) I understood: the gift portends my death.

SUBHA. Speak, man! What use will all your learning be when you are dead?

HORMAZDYAR *(delirium).* Empedocles the physician, wisest of men, spoke thus: no death, only the elements, aggregating or dissolving; opposition and affinity; Love and Discord, progenitors of Time: for while neither is stronger than the other, the world endures: undying!

A beat.

(To us) As I grew weaker I slept less and dozed more, confusing day and night, waking and dreaming. Again I saw, from the eagle's wing: sandbank and jungle and outcrop of rock black as the moon, and two slow green rivers joining forces, linking past and future. And then I knew where it derived, the gift: how second sight is sight regained: did we once speak God's language, as in a dream, transparent, the language of peacock and swan, without before or after? Then second sight *is* memory, the memory of a time before time was, no past or future.

VIRABAHU *(softly).* Hormazdyar . . .

HORMAZDYAR. Did rocks and trees speak us? Bat-blind we slept and dozed and dreamed, Saturnian, before the dawn. Leaving to God —

VIRABAHU. My lord astrologer. It is I, Virabahu.

HORMAZDYAR. . . . to see. To bear witness. *(A moment)* One night the king came and released me from my fetters, with his own hand feeding me honey.

VIRABAHU. Honey from the lion's jaws: the bees that hoard it guard my doorway.

HORMAZDYAR. Speaking gently to me, without arrogance. The armies of India were ranged below us. Ramparts breached. Lakes soiled. The pleasure gardens crowded now with sleeping soldiers, sentries, fires. By day, their engineers —

VIRABAHU. There are no armies, Hormazdyar. Go to the parapet. Look.

Almost no pause:

HORMAZDYAR. Below, the gardens, empty in the moonlight. There were no armies. Only shadows. Silence. Rain-filled fountains, dripping.

VIRABAHU. But they will come, in time.

HORMAZDYAR. In time. In our beginning was the Verb: where did
we learn this ghost-dance, time — unless from God? Below, shadows
of rock and tree. When there was no-one else to witness them, did
God choose us to share his loneliness?

A moment.

VIRABAHU. Did you see more? How did it end, your dream?

HORMAZDYAR. Strangely: a king fed me honey and called me his lord
astrologer.

Virabahu grunts.

VIRABAHU. Who can I trust, if not a man who'd rather starve to death
than feed me lies?

A moment.

Now you understand. I've been deceived before, by necromancers;
potion-mongerers; tricksters, flatterers; they come to me from China,
selling amulets, and from the West as far as Egypt, with their spells
and scarabs.

A beat.

You too are far from home, Persian. Why did you come?

HORMAZDYAR. No longer Persian. I was born in your kingdom.

VIRABAHU. But your name —

HORMAZDYAR. My name means follower of Ormazd, lord of light.

VIRABAHU. A Persian god.

HORMAZDYAR. The God of gods, creator of the world: so I was taught.
My grandfather was magus in Isfahan, under King Bahram, and sent
the youngest of his sons to Anuradhapura, to your grandfather's court,
to hear Artemides the Gnostic. And to know your grandfather, the
World-Honoured. A long journey. My father mastered many trades

before he reached the seven kingdoms, and on the road to Anuradha-pura he met a girl who quenched his thirst to travel further. They married in Hundaravapi, where they lived and died without seeing the Royal City, since she could never see it: she was blind, from birth. *(A moment)* I came to complete my father's journey.

A moment.

VIRABAHU. Tell me: do you like the girl Kalyanavati? Speak. If not—

HORMAZDYAR. I have a wife, faithful to me.

VIRABAHU. Then send for her.

HORMAZDYAR. No.

VIRABAHU. Is she like you, afraid of heights?

HORMAZDYAR. Hundaravapi is her home. *(A beat)* And mine.

VIRABAHU. But to complete your father's journey you would put your head into the lion's jaws. For that alone? No other recompense?

HORMAZDYAR. For that. And to know you, the World-Reviled.

A moment. Abruptly, a peacock cry. And with it, distantly, the slow drums announcing the dawn audience.

VIRABAHU. What do they say of me, then, in your village?

HORMAZDYAR. That fourteen years ago you stole the throne and killed your father. That your brother prince Mahinda fled to India. And that you built the Lion Fortress against his return.

More peacocks have joined in the distant cries, vying with the drums.

VIRABAHU. How little you know in Hundaravapi. *(A moment)* It seems I have much to teach *you.* What else do they say?

HORMAZDYAR. That you are a demon. And immortal.

Drums continuing. Peacock cries fading, replaced by the blowing of conches. A moment.

VIRABAHU. Sleep now. Regain your strength. You have the freedom of the rock and all its pleasures.

A beat.

But the way down, Hormazdyar: that is closed to you.

The drums and conches, growing louder, reach a climax and cease in a great fluttering of wings (as earlier — the release of doves), close now.

Then silence. Rising wind, beating against the rock, continuing as:

FA HSIEN *(close).* In the days before the siege, we lived . . . how? Not like men. Like dreamers in the halls of paradise. Remember, o my reader, what you shall never see, for it exists no longer: a king's refuge, huge-profiled like a lion, its back three acres broad and saddled with palaces, its side resplendent with painted faces, bodies: called the Wall of Heaven. On the summit, refreshed with fountain-spray, we bathed in cisterns ringed with jasmine and mimosa limpid as the sky: after the rains, the blaze of spring.

Music, distantly, wind-borne.

By night, seated on cushions in the Gem Pavilion, we watched the king dancing the story of Anandaraja, love's commissioner, while to some the golden-coloured girls dispensed favours as soft and fiery as the kiss of sherbet. I, Fa Hsien (most fortunate of guests!), was permitted to see the sacred hair relic . . . and even — touch the handkerchief that once adorned Great-Lover-Of-The-Faith, the Buddha's aunt.

Laughter, cries, with the music.

Of the advancing armies of Mahinda, the king's brother, no-one spoke. It was rumoured that they had been destroyed at sea, by storms. Some said it was not so; and that Hormazdyar the astrologer had already fled the rock. Others that he was dead at the king's hands.

Close, the tinkling of bells.

KALYANAVATI. What are you reading, master?

FA HSIEN *(continuing, to us).* Others again had seen him at the parapet, they said, at evening.

KALYANAVATI. Is it my horoscope?

HORMAZDYAR. The King's. A delicate matter: shall I follow Basilides, who allows to the progressed moon ten degrees of orb? Or Ptolemy who allows five?

Music continuing at the same distance as before; cries, laughter.

KALYANAVATI. Come, put away your work, master. This much I know: the ants only have wings in the spring. *(A beat)* I've brought you flowers. Look.

HORMAZDYAR *(close; to us:)*. Flowers: white blossom lined with red, weeping a wife's tears.

KALYANAVATI. Was I not your consort, master, in a former life?

HORMAZDYAR. What were we then? Ants?

KALYANAVATI. No.

HORMAZDYAR. Were we men?

KALYANAVATI. Not men. Geese. And we rose together, wings beating, hearts beating.

HORMAZDYAR *(different tone)*. And how far would you rise with me, Kalyanavati? From consort of the fifth rank . . . to the first? *(A moment; to us, equably)* She cursed me then: wished me among the outer barbarians, in the city of hump-backed maidens.

Music fading away, as he continues:

I was left alone, to my books and charts; Ptolemy and Basilides; to the King's chart. I knew my death and his—and could not find it in the stars.

We hear, behind his voice (and, shortly, Tissa's), a murmur, pensive:

HORMAZDYAR *(murmur)*. Saturn retrograde gives hardship in the seventh house. Hardship. Seven degrees conjunct with Mars, trine Jupiter: bids patience. If I consult Aldebaran, close to the lion's tail, will such exotics . . . no . . . Mars in the eighth, with natal Saturn, yes, but that conjunction—six degrees of orb: sudden and lingering? Or late and sudden? Mars first, by the turning of the zodiac, and yet transiting Saturn precedes. Sun in the first house, unaspected. Yet opposed to the mid-heaven. Rage against the father.

Over this, close:

HORMAZDYAR *(foreground)*. Alone? I was never alone. My door was guarded now. My evening walk, accompanied.

TISSA. I am Tissa, master, sent to watch over your safety.

HORMAZDYAR. A man of the Kulinga tribe, named for the sparrow-hawk; restless and talkative, like all his kind.

TISSA. They say that Prince Mahinda is within three days' march. Is it true? Master?

HORMAZDYAR. Above the stars reproached me: enough!

TISSA. Some say he brings a thousand men, some say ten thousand, the bravest in all India. I was his servant once, raised in his household. He and I, master, we are of an age. He will remember me. Am I foolish to think he would be merciful—if—

HORMAZDYAR. The parapet and the abyss, so close.

BLIND GIRL *(as earlier)*. This way, master. Follow me.

TISSA. But—if I fled to him, master—to Mahinda—

HORMAZDYAR. I felt the pricking at my palm. Father of heaven, shining one, celestial: let me be!

TISSA. If I go now, he might take me back: Tissa, the playmate of his youth. If I linger . . . it will be too late . . .

The background murmur ceases, with '. . . rage against the father.' Wind rising now, out of the silence.

What shall I do? For pity's sake, master, tell me!

A moment.

HORMAZDYAR. You say you were raised in Mahinda's household? He knows you as a traitor, then.

TISSA *(desperate)*. Master—

HORMAZDYAR. You were disloyal once. Be loyal now, to Virabahu.

TISSA. And shall I live? *(A moment)* How long?

HORMAZDYAR. As long as I, Tissa.

Barely a pause, and then, above the wind, the trumpeting of elephants. When they cease, an indoor acoustic, no wind:

VIRABAHU *(reading)*. Sun in the first house, unaspected, yet opposed to the mid-heaven. *(He grunts. A beat. Reading:)* Rage against the father.

A moment.

Kings have killed before. Killed fathers, mothers. Brothers. *(He pauses)* My own sister died, secretly poisoned, at my father's orders. For placing love — her chosen love — above duty. My father killed them both. Did you know that, Persian? *(A moment)* I too placed love above my filial duty — and avenged her. *(He pauses)* Rage against the father. Is this a demon's horoscope, Persian?

HORMAZDYAR. A man's.

VIRABAHU. A man's? A king's rather. It foreshows me as I am.

HORMAZDYAR. No.

VIRABAHU. I've been told it a hundred times —

HORMAZDYAR. By flatterers. King or beggar, the stars are indifferent to office. Only danger, conflict, and delight: these three are pre-ordained. The several paths a man may take; but not —

VIRABAHU *(interrupts)*. By divination, then —

HORMAZDYAR. Comes augury. *(A beat)* A crow riding on an ox, good fortune, but the heron, crying twice, denies it. These are lessons in making ready: ox, crow, and heron: be with them, no more, no less. Our own design is gossamer, as fragile as a spider's web.

VIRABAHU. And as certain.

HORMAZDYAR. Never certain. Wind and rain destroy its fabric. A way of knowing leads like footprints to the water's edge, bringing the sea closer: if each wave had a name, should we be wiser?

A beat.

VIRABAHU. My sister had a name: Dayal Bati. But do they tell her story in your village? Your wise men—do they say how I avenged her? No. I tell you, Persian, when I defeat my brother I shall capture him alive and make him speak the truth, for all to know.

A moment.

You talk of making ready. Fourteen years I have been waiting for Mahinda, making everything secure, and now a favourable planet draws him to me like the quarry to the crouching lion. Can't you see it in your charts, this planet? Saturn—

HORMAZDYAR. In the Scorpion's house. Beware. From Saturn we learn patience, or we suffer. Sometimes it hovers, and goes backward: this is dangerous, if you go out to battle.

VIRABAHU. Then I shall wait for augury.

A moment.

What do you say, astrologer?

HORMAZDYAR. You *must* go out. Unless you can withstand a siege.

VIRABAHU (*grunts, amused*). Ah but I can.

HORMAZDYAR. How long?

VIRABAHU. Longer than Saturn retrograde.

A moment.

As long as rock is rock, and water flows through stone-carved hollows in the earth, feeding the palace wells out of a secret channel. Where its source is: where the spring rises: only I know. Those who devised and built the water-course I buried with it. Have no fear, Hormazdyar, we are safe here on the rock.

A beat.

HORMAZDYAR (*close; to us*). On the rock. Secure as gods, but gods who can never descend and take a human shape. Secure as ghosts.

The trumpeting of war elephants; rousing the peacocks of the rock. The cries compete, across each other, fading as Hormazdyar resumes:

Below us range Mahinda's armies, with their canopies and banners. As I foresaw it: ramparts breached, lakes soiled, the pleasure gardens crowded now with sleeping soldiers, sentries, fires. From the Lion Rock we watch them wake and dress to practise shadow wars; we watch them eat and bathe their elephants and settle to sleep again; watching, God's ghost companions, haunting his kingdom. *(A beat)* And every night I dreamt of Arrow Fountain, far across the plain.

Hum of bees, close, angry. Fading slowly.

Still Saturn frowned. My friend Fa Hsien the pilgrim, the devout, suffered his anger, while seeking to flee the rock: instead he met a swarm of bees roused by Mahinda's engineers.

Close: a groan, or stifled yelp.

Hold still, Fa Hsien. Think of the Noble Eightfold Path.

Fa Hsien yelps again.

I drew the stings, and rubbed in balm. *(To Fa Hsien)* Remember: life, the Buddha says, consists of irreality, impermanence, and misery. Life is pain.

Fa Hsien groans agreement.

FA HSIEN. Better not to be born, then.

HORMAZDYAR. Freedom must be earned.

FA HSIEN. Why?

HORMAZDYAR. Such is karma: would you rather be at the whim of gods and demons?

FA HSIEN. Is it better to be confined to a rock, at the mercy of warring brothers? Today I watched Mahinda's men sully the shrine in the Garden of Gold and use the sacred bo-tree for firewood! I've prayed beneath that tree — prayed —

HORMAZDYAR (*interrupting*). You will see Canton again. Picture it—and be still. (*Over Fa Hsien's yelps:*) Last night I dreamt a pious dream, of a bo-tree whose branches sank into the earth to rise again; and a spring called Arrow Fountain whose waters sank and rose again, in my dream, to refresh heaven.

FA HSIEN. You saw Nirvana?

HORMAZDYAR. No, an earthly heaven. You may offer thanks there, Fa Hsien, for your safety. (*Close, to us:*) And I told him of the grove called Sight Regained.

A beat.

FA HSIEN. Where is this place?

HORMAZDYAR. On the road to Anuradhapura. Where my father met a blind girl: my mother. And I too—

GIRL (*as earlier*). This way, master. Follow me.

HORMAZDYAR. I too was taken by the hand and learnt to see.

GIRL. From here you can see Fire Domain, and Arrow Fountain where the stream rises. Shall I fetch you some water?

HORMAZDYAR. And she led me out of the grove, never once letting go of my hand, across the broad-planked bridge, towards the house.

Barely a pause:

FA HSIEN. That night, restored by the powers of the King's magus Hormazdyar, I made good my escape. As in former times when brick and wood were raised by rope, to build the pavilions at the summit: so by rope I now descended, invisible to the palace and its guards standing motionless in their rocky alcoves, gazing at the firelit armies below. A long descent: my body pressed against the painted bodies on the fabled Wall of Heaven.

One distant peacock cry.

In our intimacy, their nakedness made me visible from afar: it was their undoing, and mine: at the foot of the rock Mahinda himself awaited me.

Gradually, more peacock cries.

What I, a poor pilgrim, a devotee of relics, had seen; what I have told *you*, my reader: this I told the Prince, and under threat of death could tell no more—neither the might of Virabahu's armoury nor the sum of his provisions nor yet the secret of which Mahinda spoke to me, concerning a hidden channel that fed the palace wells from far across the plain: where its source was: where the spring rose.

Drums, distant, beginning.

If I could lead him to it, I might be spared. If not, I would pay for what I had seen; with my eyes.

Blowing of conches, over the drums.

And I remembered what Hormazdyar himself had told me, of a spring whose waters sank into the earth and rose again, in his dream, to refresh heaven: Arrow Fountain, on the road to Anuradhapura. And the grove called Sight Regained.

A moment's silence, then the fluttering release of doves, close.

HORMAZDYAR *(as earlier)*. A place to offer thanks, Fa Hsien, for your safety.

FA HSIEN. There Prince Mahinda set me free. For indeed: it was the place.

Wind rising. Distantly, Subha's proclamation: 'Virabahu, the World-Honoured, the Conqueror . . .'

HORMAZDYAR *(close; brokenly)*. A dream. Spoken in ignorance. And now I saw their deaths, as if before me, on the bridge called Force-of-Arms: a bearded man, a blind girl. *(A beat)* I saw the watercourse exposed, the channel dry. A drought on the Lion Rock. A king goes down to battle. Great Ormazd—

VIRABAHU. Is this the day? Hormazdyar of Hundaravapi, step forward.

HORMAZDYAR *(to us, as before)*. A king goes down—

VIRABAHU. What do you say, my bird of omen?

Hormazdyar answers firmly, loud:

HORMAZDYAR. That you can wait no longer.

VIRABAHU. And shall I triumph?

A moment.

HORMAZDYAR (*to us*). Great Ormazd, is this your will? Below me, death winnows a field of men. The world that keeps us from the world — did I hope to see it from the Lion Rock, so *much* of the world that —

VIRABAHU. Speak! Is Saturn in the Scorpion's house?

HORMAZDYAR. It is.

VIRABAHU. Is it the day ordained? Shall I scatter Mahinda's forces?

A moment.

HORMAZDYAR. Yes, great king! Like seed before the wind.

A many-throated shout, above the wind.

VIRABAHU (*closer; to Hormazdyar alone*). Am I not immortal, Persian?

HORMAZDYAR. Yes; immortal.

Drums: and, slowly rising, the distant cries of battle. The trumpeting of war elephants.

(*close; to us*) Time: it seems so small a thing, now it is in my gift. Would it have come to be, this day, if I had never spoken? Tricked by a dream: had I come, then, not to speak the future, nor to tell the stars: not to serve the Lion Throne but to destroy it; seeing everything, and knowing nothing?

Battle cries, closer. A beat.

Or was all yet in the balance? The day, the contest: by one gleam of distant Aldebaran —

FA HSIEN (*no pause*). Unknown to all, Virabahu had built a chamber in the lower rock and into it, before the siege began, withdrawn his elephants. Great was the terror in Mahinda's forces when they saw the God-king ride out from the belly of the Lion, on an elephant armoured for war. No less did this inflame the spirits of his own soldiers, who fought more like demons than men, driving Mahinda back across the trampled causeways of the pleasure gardens, over a field of dead and drowning men, filling the lakes and shallow pools with blood; almost to the outer ramparts.

Sounds of battle continuing, at the same distance. Wind audible, closer.

TISSA *(close)*. Master, rejoice.

HORMAZDYAR. Rejoice?

TISSA. The day is won.

HORMAZDYAR. Not yet, Tissa.

TISSA *(after a moment)*. Know then: if we lose, I am to throw you from the rock.

A moment. Battle cries continuing.

FA HSIEN. Others have written: having breached the last line of his brother's foot-soldiers, the Lion King rode on, beyond the ramparts, into the jungle, and was seen no more; there he still awaits his forces, on a saddle of red silk, riding an elephant whose oaken legs shine with the blood of Indian soldiers.

A moment.

FA HSIEN. But I, Fa Hsien, will not indulge the credulous. I write for the serene joy and emotion of the pious. Great is karma; humble its instruments; dreadful the end of one who killed his father and proclaimed himself immortal.

HORMAZDYAR *(close; brokenly)*. Pull back the mask, the veil of maya, to show . . . what? A darkness. Or a rotting face? Fleshwires, blood and sinew? *(A beat)* Too late I recalled their deaths, on the bridge called Force-of-Arms: a bearded man, a blind girl.

FA HSIEN. As King Virabahu approached the outer rampart by a narrow causeway, long familiar to him, but now sullied and breached by the invaders, he came upon a gap no wider than a man might jump, yet too wide for his elephant to cross: on such mischances are empires lost and won. For then, seeing the God-king turn his elephant, Virabahu's soldiers paused in fear, and fell back before Mahinda's charge. *(A moment)* The Lion King watched from his mount, alone. With my own eyes I saw him draw his sword, raise it, drive it home into his breast, raise it again to heaven; and replace it in its scabbard; before falling dead across his saddle.

A moment. Cries fading now.

Slaughter followed, and the burning of the palaces, they say, was visible from India itself. With it the Lion Throne has passed from sight. If travellers can be believed, the jungle has already claimed the pleasure gardens and the rock, to throttle it with vines. *(He pauses)* All these things happened in my youth. My wanderings had only just begun.

The cries have ceased, leaving only the wind, beating at the rock.

TISSA. Master . . . master, you could have saved yourself, and me.

HORMAZDYAR. No, Tissa.

TISSA. You told me to stay. *(A moment)* Said I would live.

HORMAZDYAR. As long as I. *(A beat)* Will you obey a dead king?

TISSA. A defeated king, master. His servants are dead men now.

A moment.

Look your last. Then die, as I must.

HORMAZDYAR *(to us)*. I looked. Above the battlefield, smoke coiled like a serpent: a dragon made visible. *(A beat; to Tissa)* Are you not afraid?

TISSA. Yes.

A moment. A lone peacock cry, alarmed.

HORMAZDYAR. Think: we are between heaven and earth. One step over the parapet, and death vanishes.

TISSA. Help me, master.

HORMAZDYAR. Think: we are between heaven and earth. One step over the parapet, and death vanishes.

TISSA. Help me, master.

HORMAZDYAR. Take my hand.

TISSA. Have you no fear, then?

HORMAZDYAR. Not of dying.

More peacock cries, distantly.

(Close, to us) But I was afraid: to see the rotting face behind the veil.

Rising, louder than the peacocks, closer: angry bees.

And then we heard it — like the rising spirits of the dead, tormented —

TISSA. Master!

Bees, closer.

HORMAZDYAR. Come. Now —

A moment. Bees, close.

(close) Ormazd: accept my soul.

A cry, Tissa's. Rushing of wind; the bees fading.

(close) Together, falling. *(A beat)* Drowning in air.

The wind fades, ceases. Silence.

A darkness. Fear, but no pain.

A pause. Then:

GIRL. Stay close. It's darker still for me, master. But I know the way.

Gradually, from a distance, the sound of the flute, from the house hidden by trees. A moment.

From here you can see Fire Domain, and Arrow Fountain where the stream rises. Shall I fetch you some water?

HORMAZDYAR. And she led me out of the grove, never once letting go of my hand, across the broad-planked bridge, towards my father's house.

The flute continuing, rising gradually in volume, across the closing credits.

❧

THE SEA VOYAGE

or,
The Travels *and* Ultramarine Adventures
of Don Juan Hurtado de la Vega,
Knight Commander
Of the Order of St James;

being his Two Years' Voyage *begun* 1527 *from Sanlucar in Spain, to* Malucho, *as some say the* Spice Islands; *the fleet having to pass the strait of* Magellan; *with the* Memorable Heroism *of the Captain-General; his* blasphemous Descent *into* Folly & Sad End *upon the* Isle of Candigar; *with the* Singular Testimonies *of his* Murderer, *Fray Simon of Cordova, chaplain to the fleet;* a True Relation *drawing copiously upon the late* Discoveries *in* Manilla; *translated and assembled* by
Carey Harrison, Gent.

Part One: VOYAMALUCO!

For Gert Hofmann

Preface

The Sea Voyage was commissioned in 1973 (between commission and delivery a BBC-record-breaking 16 years went by on research, writing and rewriting; and on other, intervening projects); the play was born five years earlier still, in '68, on the night of the first moon landing. Seeing the surface of the moon, on television; and the moon in the night sky, outside the window; and reflecting that the American explorers in their lunar suits might as well have been in a simulator as on the moon itself—not only for all *we* would have known, but for all *they* would have known, so thoroughly mediated was their experience of the bodily immediacies of exploration: the ordeals by jungle, desert, and ocean that were intrinsic to its history. Intrinsic? Or only incidental? Perhaps the imperative of exploration was still being met by this grail quest in helmet and pressurized suit. There was still plenty of danger. And conspicuous, if not obscene, expense. Imperial interests were being served. Yet: something more than greed, too; and more than curiosity. Exploration (as opposed to migration) . . . akin perhaps to pilgrimage? And with this thought came, in time, the idea of a search for the bones of Christ: the ultimate relic. An imaginary fleet—a visionary conquistador (or one seduced by heresy)—mortification of the flesh . . . and a good deal of patience on the part of the BBC. The bones of Christ: at every turn I expected to be told that, as a hypothetical grail, this was absurd. I wasn't; but it is, of course. Christ's bones: a contradiction, and a conjunction—flesh and spirit, God and man: conjunct *and* contradictory. Bringing together all the issues that propel the play: Gnosticism and the belief that flesh is a necessary but loathsome mistake, the work of a misbegotten demiurge; pilgrimage and mortification of the flesh, those ordeals by desert, jungle, ocean . . . obstinately peopled (as St Jerome found) by our more familiar longings, dreams, fantasies; and finally paganism, a glowing core still present in a Catholic Church riven by corruption and—at the time of our imaginary journey—about to give birth to a joyless, self-sufficient, European child: Protestantism. Imagine, then, a bunch of European renegades; cast-offs and desperadoes; surrounded by their cargo, physical and metaphysical; adrift month after month on an immense uncharted ocean, until deprived at last of time itself, as of *their* very self; hallucinating a kind of history—what's left of it—of the European imagination, their involuntary baggage. In the middle of the Pacific, the last stand of the ecstatic European.

Voyamaluco!, Part One of *The Sea Voyage*, was first broadcast on BBC Radio 3 on May 9 1989. The cast was as follows:

JUAN HURTADO DE LA VEGA	Philip Voss
SIMÓN PÉREZ	John McAndrew
MANILIUS	Norman Rodway
GERÓNIMO BERNÁLDEZ	Trevor Peacock
SANTIAGO DE MORGA	Norman Jones
MELCHIOR ALEMÁN	Struan Rodger
SULEIMAN THE MAGNIFICENT	Sam Dale
ALEJANDRO DE LA CUEVA	David Sinclair
ALONSO NIÑO	Joe Dunlop
TOMÁS DE GÁLVEZ	Donald Gee
PERALONSO MÉNDEZ	Christopher Good
DON FELIPE (PRINCE ZULA)	Sam Dale
IRISH STEVE	Ken Cumberledge
CHARLES V	Francis Middleditch
RECRUITING OFFICER	William Simons
PEDAGOGIC PEPPER POD	Sam Dale
SAND-CLOCK BOY	Clive Samways
WHORES and LADIES OF THE COURT	Alice Arnold, Jo Kendall Marcia King, and Joan Walker
SCHOOLBOYS and ORPHAN BOYS	Oliver Bailey, Nicholas Biskins, Stephen Evans, Alan Forster, Simon Mead, Alexis Roxborough, Clive Samways, and James Thomas, from Dulwich College

PIRATES, VENETIANS, ALBANIANS, CAMELS, TRADERS OF SEVILLE, ARMOURERS OF SPAIN, QUARTERMASTER'S MEN, OLD SALTS, GRANDEES, DUKES, DUCHESSES, CAPTAINS, SHIP'S OFFICERS, and other parts, were played by members of the cast.

Director: Jane Morgan

Lapping waves and, distantly, the Salve Regina, the ancient hymn sung every evening by the seaborne conquistadores. Their untrained, raucous, unaccompanied voices swell and fade on the wind.

1ST NARRATOR. This is the story of the Fourth Armada to the Isles of Spice; of Juan Hurtado de la Vega, its commander, and the men who sailed with him, in 1527, from the Dock of Mules, Seville, to the uncharted archipelagoes of the Great South Sea: el mar Pacífico. What they would find there, other than spice, no-one could yet be sure. Only seven years earlier, Magellan had found 'el paso', the narrow strait breaching the southern tip of South America, and sailed through it into an ocean full of islands. Beyond them, surely, lay Cipangu—fabulous China. Beyond it, biblical Tarshish and the golden port of Ophir, source of Solomon's wealth; beyond these the lost Christian realm of Presbyter John, Lord of Hither Ind, land of the dreaded Gog and Magog, and the Ten Lost Tribes. And the worm Salamander. And Amazons and Brahmins. And paradise and pearls and pepper.

2ND NARRATOR. Above all, pepper. To cure meat, and keep the taste of rotting flesh from European tongues. Salt was readily available, but the Spice Islands sent pepper west along a chain of middlemen whose ever greedier demands made the price a standing joke. And the journey was a dangerous one, fraught with adventures exotic enough to match those told by the conquistadores...

The hymn has faded, to be replaced by the noise of a dockside crowd.

THE PEDAGOGIC PEPPER POD (*oriental; dry*). I am a pepper pod.

VOICE FROM THE CROWD. A pepperpot?

P.P.POD. A pepper *pod*. A *bean*.

2ND VOICE. *Where* yo' been?

P.P.POD. Ah been to a port on de Red Sea . . .

3RD VOICE. Jiddah?

P.P.POD. Never laid hands on her. *(Above laughter)* Now listen: I was picked and sorted, dried and baled, in the Moluccas. And bought for a pittance by a Malay merchant—

MALAY MERCHANT *(softly)*. Dis is Molucca day!

P.P.POD. Then sailed by junk to the Malay peninsula—

Warcries, splashes.

We fought off the usual Chinese pirates—

CHINESE PIRATE *(distantly)*. Pepper pod, you die!

He falls in.

P.P.POD. The Malay merchant sold me to a Hindoo trader; he paid a heavy tax to the Sultan of Malacca—

Coins; voices.

HINDOO TRADER. The tax, your Heaviness.

P.P.POD. We sailed for Calicut—

Distantly, warcries; splashes.

P.P.POD. Fighting off pirates in the Bay of Bengal. At Calicut, in the Emporium . . .

Hubbub of the Emporium.

HINDOO TRADER. I sold the pepper at a handsome profit to an ugly fellow from the backside of Africa: Abyssinia.

ABYSSINIAN MERCHANT *(glum)*. Not if I see you first.

P.P.POD. He too paid tariffs to the local potentates. We sailed for Egypt—this time in an Arab convoy. And this time Indian pirates came at us in a whole squadron of little zambucos.

Shouts; splashes.

Much cargo was lost. From Jiddah on the Red Sea we were given an escort of black spearmen to take us to the Egyptian border. By camel we travelled to Alexandria; by caravan to Beirut.

Grunts, plodding; cries.

Seventy beasts, grunting and swaying in the dust, roped head to tail, led slowly by an ass. At each oasis a sheikh to be paid, an emir to be bribed, an ass to be watered. In between each oasis, dunes; behind the dunes, robbers.

Whispers, stealthy movement.

Sometimes the guards went mad. In the desert, music steals from underneath the dunes . . .

Faint, high-pitched laughter, and a rattling tambourine.

By night, the crash of ghostly drums. By day the spectral cavalcades: the remnants of forgotten peoples toiling on the skyline; whole cities sand-smothered in a night and turned to stone. We passed them; they were open to the air, guarded by jackals. The bazaars of stone, the craftsmen, dancers, jugglers and musicians with their gleaming timbrels, all of stone. Silkworms of stone, in petrified mulberry boughs.

Faint, high laughter.

We passed on. In Alexandria the Sultan of Egypt, a dwarf, took a full third of the asking price, as tribute.

THE SULTAN. It's not too much to ask, surely? How else will you Venetians get your pepper?

THE VENETIANS *(resignedly)*. How indeed, your Dwarfishness?

P.P.POD. By galley now, we shipped for Venice. Ah, the calm Mediterranean! Safe at last.

Warcries, splashes.

I'd forgotten the Ottoman warships! The blockade! Hands off, you filthy Turk!

TRIPOLI CORSAIR. I'm not a filthy Turk. I'm a filthy Tripoli corsair!

Falls in, with a whoop. Shouts fading.

P.P.POD. And even in sight of Venice, the Albanians swarmed out at night, to board us . . .

THE ALBANIANS. Shhh!

A moment's hush, then cries, whoops, and fighting, fading away.

P.P.POD. We survivors were relieved, and proud, to stand on the Rialto. After all this danger, all this bribery and bakshish, double-dealing on the bumcheeks of the world, small wonder if the bale that cost a ducat in Malacca fetched a hundred in Vienna or Bruges . . .

MERCHANT OF BRUGES. Zut! 'Ow much?

P.P.POD. Only ten thousand per cent, my friend. Bon appetit!

A gulp — as price and pod are swallowed.

1ST NARRATOR. Europeans swallowed price and pod. But what if there were a cheaper route? The survivors of Magellan's expedition circumnavigated the globe and returned with pepper. Charles of Spain sent out Armadas in their wake. Seven years passed. Not a ship returned. 'El paso' was beginning to get a bad name; it was too cold; too dangerous; it was blocked altogether (some said) by a huge rock, newly tempest-torn from the Tierra del Fuego; it was attended (some said) by Leviathan, greatest of things that swim . . . and Charles, now Holy Roman Emperor, had other fish to fry.

Rising sound of court chatter.

Naples was giving trouble, yet again; the whole of Italy was giving trouble; and the Grand Turk was marching on Vienna. Money, as always, was in short supply — the imperial throne had cost a fortune in electoral bribes. Fleets were costly; this Molucco or Maluco was too far away; and Suleiman, Suleiman the Magnificent, was marching on Vienna.

2ND NARRATOR. Then came Hurtado. Juan Hurtado. A soldier. He had fought at Pavia and figured, it seems, in a seaborne raid on Tunis. A mercenary on occasion; but for a well-born soldier this was becoming increasingly respectable.

Booted footsteps on marble, approaching steadily. Distant proclamations.

Well-born he was, and well-connected both at church and court. He was no seaman — unless we count the Tunis adventure — but to be made Captain-General of an Armada it was enough to be a noble Castilian with money to help finance the expedition; and his own reasons for going . . .

CHAMBERLAIN. Don Juan Hurtado de la Vega.

A hush.

HURTADO. Sire.

CHARLES V. Don Juan. *(He pauses)* Magellan, Loaysa, Saavedra: all dead. Must I lose more knights of Santiago to the Great Green, to the sharks? A *Fourth* Armada to the Isles of Spice? Why?

Murmurs. They fall silent.

Well?

HURTADO *(to us)*. One does not speak of pepper to an Emperor. *(Loud)* Sire! Does not the psalmist sing 'The Kings of Tarshish and the Isles shall bring presents; the Kings of Sheba and Saba shall offer gifts . . . then shalt thou lay up gold as dust, and the Gold of Ophir as the stones of the brooks . . .' Did not my lord Elcano see with his own eyes the mines of Cipangu, its nuggets big as walnuts — bigger — big as eggs! The wealth of Oriental China belongs to your Christian Majesty, by right!

Approving murmurs, in the echoing hall.

CHARLES V. The King of Portugal has claimed that Oriental China lies in *his* domain . . .

HURTADO. The King of Portugal has yet to *discover* Oriental China.

A GEOGRAPHER *(very old)*. Sire, by my globe . . . to the south and west of Banguey in the Sulu Sea lie John of Portugal's possessions. Cipangu, to the north and west (as we believe), is Spain's . . .

CHARLES V. Perhaps.

HURTADO *(to us)*. He muses. The Emperor muses. A fleet, against a thousand bales of pepper . . . and the odds? With sixteen ships already lost? Cheaper to buy from the Venetians. As for the gold of China . . . well, not even Charles believes in that. He has, I know, a plan to *sell* his Oriental spiceries to Portugal, for coin: coin to outfit an army, and oppose the Turk. Why send more ships to these remote, unprofitable islands . . . (*a moment*) unless . . . and now he sees it! To imply some secret information confirming the reports of treasure and so add, perhaps, two hundred thousand ducats to the price of these Moluccas or Maluchoes, call them what you like . . . sell 'em to Portugal! The stratagem pleases. First send Hurtado! That'll make the Portuguese sit up. Would Charles send Juan Hurtado into the jaws of death on a fool's errand? Never! Not Juan Hurtado, that hero belov'd of Spain!

Rising, in an outdoor acoustic, schoolyard cries.

For, yes . . . I am belov'd. I am a hero. Every schoolboy knows 'The Feats Of Juan Hurtado': they learn it in the classroom!

Two sharp taps on blackboard slate, hushing the class.

A SCHOOLMASTER. Martín!

MARTÍN (*aged 12; rises noisily to his feet*). 'The Feats Of Juan Hurtado de la Vega'. By Antonio César.

HURTADO. A distant relative of mine. I paid him well.

MARTÍN. 'In May the Janissaries marched
          Against Bohemia. Louis of Hungary
          Was trembling as I stood before him,
          Bearing orders from the Emperor!
          We left Shabotz to Suleiman
          On the Eighth of July —
          But we disputed Belgrade! As
          The world knows, and Suleiman!
          Suleiman, Selim's son,
          The lesser soldier but the greater man
          (He kept his word at Rhodes, by Seth!
          When the Grandmaster sued for peace).
          I fought this warrior
          And poet, Lord of Lords —'

SCHOOLMASTER (*interrupting*). Bartolomé!

BARTOLOMÉ (*promptly*). ' — in the Carpathians,
          Vlad the Impaler at my side

And Young Szapolyi The Effeminate
And the Ban of Banát. We were taken at last
At Mitrovitz, that sea-cold fortress,
Where I spoke with Suleiman
Beneath the pines, and won my freedom.
But John, young John,
John the traitor,
Vassal King of Transylvania —'

Around Bartolomé, noise rising, suppressed, anticipatory —

'He yielded to the Turk . . .'

And now classroom delight at the deliberate, suggestive emphasis.

SCHOOLMASTER. Silence!

BARTOLOMÉ *(continuing)*. 'For many years
Wallachia entreated my return.
While I, with a handful of arquebusiers —'

SCHOOLMASTER. Felipe!

FELIPE. '. . . was salting Barbarossa's tail,
Till Suleiman himself came forth
One April morning from Constantinople,
Eighty thousand strong. Louis of Hungary
Was slow, that weak Bohemian.
Who else but Vlad the Devil,
And the Ban, and I,
Braved the Ottoman at Mohacs, on the plain!
The Transylvanians advanced, we met them
With a cannonade and charged
The first line with the heavy cavalry.
We *broke* the feudal serfs! Too well —
Our guns were slow to follow.
When the Janissaries struck us
From the right, we drove them off
And smashed the second line — but
The artillery! They chained their cannon
Together, by the grey Danube.

> We could not pierce their cannon,
> On the plain of Mohacs. By Santiago!
> Seven Bishops died that day!

HURTADO. And a whole herd of princelings. True. I earned my wages, at Mohacs. True, that I spoke with Suleiman, at Mitrovitz. And that soft summer's day beneath the pines: that day: my expedition to the Isles of Spice was born.

Outdoor acoustic: wind in the trees and soft Turkish strings and a tambourine.

I was held to ransom there all summer in the castle, betrayed by the Sultan's bumboy John. Suleiman came. We walked in the woods, and spoke of God, and danced the zumba in the courtyard, he and I.

SULEIMAN *(fond, sly)*. Don Juan. Don Juan Hurtado de la Vega. Don Juanito.

HURTADO. As token of his love I had from him a heron's feather and a manuscript of the Eight Evil Thoughts, the lost apophthegms of Evagrius Ponticus. And, in Suleiman's own hand, The Testament of Nestor, a famed hermit of antiquity.

SULEIMAN. Read it, my friend. Memorize it.

HURTADO. Reading, I knew at once that Seth himself, immortal ancestor, had sent Suleiman to me, and with him this precious guide to our true Christian story. I knew that I was born to fulfil Nestor's wish, and retrieve from the Orient a treasure more glorious than any dreamed of by a Christian king. A treasure buried, like old Adam, to the east of Paradise: the bones of Christ our Lord!

Abrupt, thunderous, in a church acoustic, with organ accompaniment:

CHORUS. Laus Deo!

In the echoing silence that follows:

HURTADO *(meditative)*. The bones of Christ.

The murmurs of Charles' court return.

CHARLES V. Don Juan Hurtado de la Vega, we are informed that you have undertaken to assist your Sovereign, with your own means, to equip a Fourth Armada to the Isles of Spice; your Emperor looks favourably on your valorous request. Inasmuch as it lies in our power we shall assist you; and ourselves draw up the regulations for this journey in our name. Praise be to God, that sends Spain such sons! Laus Deo!

THE COURT. Laus Deo!

Clamorous applause, fading.

HURTADO. Praise be to God; and greed. I knew that as soon as we had sailed Charles would begin negotiations with the King of Portugal; that we would reach the China Seas only to find ourselves in Portuguese waters. These things I could not tell my crew. But for myself I had no fears; to find that of which old Nestor the Mesopotamian had written I would have braved the might of Arab, Turk, and Portuguese at once. Nestor! Old anchorite: my guide!

Soft plangent Moorish music. And, faintly, water lapping at the dock.

In Cádiz where I knew the mariners, I found my ships. Waterfront gossip, not the lies of ship-owners, led me to the best; or shall we say the least maligned. The smallest, the San Gil, known as —

SEAMAN 1. La Cucaracha!

HURTADO. Cockroach. Because of her speed.

SEAMAN 1 *(belches, sceptical)*. Pardon me.

HURTADO. Next, the San Cristóbal. Called —

SEAMAN 2. La Culada!

SEAMAN 3. Boot-Up-The-Arse . . .

HURTADO. Because of her handling characteristics.

SEAMAN 4 *(chortling)*. Because of her —

A hand is clapped across his mouth.

SEAMAN 5 *(drily)*. Called Up-Your-Arse, after a certain —

DOMINGO VÉLEZ *(ghostly)*. Domingo Vélez, ship's carpenter. Hanged off the Cape of the Eleven Thousand Virgins.

SHIP'S OFFICER. For sodomy!

OMNES. May God receive his soul!

DOMINGO VÉLEZ (*urgently*). And when they throw my body on the great waters, Lord, let me sink with my face upwards, raised to thee!

SHIP'S CHAPLAIN. Amen.

HURTADO. The fine ship Santa María La Blanca, caravel! Variously called —

SEAMAN 1. La Vaca!

HURTADO. Cow.

SEAMAN 2. Rocín de madera!

HURTADO. Wooden horse.

SEAMAN 3. Pájaro puerco!

HURTADO. Flying pig.

SEAMAN 4 (*ancient*). I call her . . . Cacaplata. Shit-Silver!

Hoots and laughter.

HURTADO (*sternly*). The Ysabel. Known as —

SEAMAN 5. La Bomba!

HURTADO. The Pump.

SEAMAN 5 (*ribald*). Why?

OMNES. Because her pump sucks like an old whore from Valencia!

HURTADO. And finally . . . the flagship! Nuestra Señora del Buen Aire. Our Lady of the Fair Wind!

A moment as the seamen fight to stifle laughter; and win.

OMNES (*hearty*). Laus Deo!

SEAMAN (*pious; quietly:*) Praise be to God.

Music fading; slowly rising dockside bustle, as provisioning begins.

HURTADO.   Five sturdy clumsy ships, lateen-rigged to bend a breeze around.   Not one had seen the hurricane or fled bare-poled before an equinoctial storm.   The broma and the teredos, worms of the torrid zone, would make short work of these: I had them brought up to Seville and there hove down and graved; their bottoms pitched; seams payed; rigged square, and readied for three years at sea.

In the background, groans of wood, wheels, and men.   Muleteers' cries.

Beside them on the Dock of Mules stood our provisions, mountainous. The Emperor sent errand-boys with idle promises of money; and a whining quartermaster; I dismissed him and installed my own. I bought the stores myself, although it beggared me. The bales and boxes spread across the key as though Europe itself were setting out for undiscovered Cipangu.   Mustard, sugar, vinegar, salt, rice, flour, raisins, figs, onions, capers: the traders of Seville fell over themselves to meet our needs...

THE TRADERS OF SEVILLE   *(distantly audible behind Hurtado's narration; singly — ever more glad —).*   Two hundred and seventy-three thousand pounds of biscuit, your Magnificence —
One thousand and fifty cheeses —
Six hundred and twenty butts of Sherry wine —
Two and a quarter tons of olive oil —
Two hundred and forty barrels of anchovies —
Four hundred and sixty large dried fish —
Two tons of beans —
Three tons of chick peas —
Two and a half tons of dried pork —
Three hundred and fifty strings of garlic —
Fifteen hundredweight of almonds in their shells —
Honey and currants and quince jelly for the Captain-General . . .

HURTADO *(above this)*.   And seven cows and three pigs living jostling in the hold beside the bales of cheap cloth; yellow kerchiefs to delight the Indians; coloured buckram by the ton; eight thousand common red caps; and three coloured velvets for Indian persons of dignity. With fifty scissors to help them divide Mine from Thine. And to protect it, four thousand eight hundred German knives.

Soft cries; crashes; laughter, rising.

Nine hundred looking-glasses to amuse, and frighten. Bracelets, and basins; combs; unguents; perfumes; oils, and salves, to keep the New World bright and clean. And twenty thousand little bells; hawks' bells; to make it tinkle.

Bells, laughter. Silence.

There would be some tribes not so easily flattered. And some encounters called for other arguments. And then, there were the Portuguese. The other arguments included—

THE ARMOURERS OF SPAIN. Sixty crossbows, with four thousand three hundred and twenty arrows and a hundred skeins of crossbow wire—
One thousand and forty darts—
Ten dozen javelins—
A thousand lances—

HURTADO. More or less; some never came, from Biscay. And more were stolen on the dock . . .

THE ARMOURERS OF SPAIN (*continuing distantly, across each other, while Hurtado continues*). Pikes—Boarding pikes—Bilbao shields—Fifty arquebuses with flasks and prickers and four hundred foot of fuse—a hundred corselets, armlets, shoulderplates and helmets, and a hundred breastplates with throatpieces, and with helmets—Two suits of armour for the Captain-General, a coat of mail and seven swordblades—

HURTADO. We loaded sixteen pounds of emery and leathers, to clean the weapons and the armour. And I saw to it myself that the ships sported new culverins, falconets, bombards, pasamuros; shot and cannonballs of iron and stone; and just over five thousand pounds of gunpowder.

THE QUARTERMASTER'S MEN (*behind Hurtado; across each other; crescendo:*). Eighty flags; two of them taffeta. Eighty-nine lanterns. Five anchors each per ship. Rope; nails; planks; oakum; grease; tar; pitch; awls; needles; resin; canvas. Spare yards; pulleys; spars; blocks. Six cauldrons. Two ovens. Grindstones; an anvil; and a forge—

HURTADO *(over them)*. It was the pride of Spain: the finest fleet and the most lavishly equipped that ever was assembled at the Dock of Mules . . .

THE QUARTERMASTER'S MEN *(from all directions)*. Forty-two pint measures, present and correct! Pots; ladles; knives; trenchers; mess bowls; porringers; choppers; platters! Fifty-six iron pikes and hammers! Pincers; mallets; boathooks; seines; fishing lines; floats; chain hooks; harpoons; spears! And ten thousand five hundred fish hooks! Sir!

Silence.

HURTADO. And two hundred and fifty men, in five ships thirteen paces long, for three years. With this in mind: handcuffs, irons, padlocks, and chains were included. Spades; pickaxes; to dig, among other things, important graves. The unimportant could be trusted to the sea. And for the chaplain of the fleet: furniture to pray for their salvation.

Thunderous, the opening of the Vexilla Regis. Full choir. Then silence.

Two hundred and fifty men. In five ships thirteen paces long. For three years.

The Vexilla Regis resumes, a dark, low chant.

Taffeta flags and Sherry wine could be bought, for such a journey. But men? Voyamaluco: I'm going to Maluco! The bravest had sailed before, and one in five returned to tell a grim tale: three years on a forty-footer with a single cabin, the captain's; and fifty blistered brawling frightened men. When seas ran high they crawled down and shat in the bilgewater, alive with rats; and hardened sailors fainted at the stink. They lived ate slept huddled on deck. Two of the three years in uncharted waters. Landfall meant reefs; no landfall, starvation. One in five the chances of survival. My own friends fled to their estates in case I asked them to ship with me. But men — certain men — were to be had, at a price. Four sea captains —

ROJAS. Hernando Rojas.

DE SORIA. Rafael de Soria, el mozo.

DE ESTRADA. Don Jorge de Estrada.

RUIZ. Rodrigo Ruiz de Trassierra.

HURTADO. —needed the pay, urgently. Half in advance. Ruiz owed money. Rojas bought himself out of prison. They all received coin; a crack at fame and fortune; a ship each, and a cabin. To the officers on my own ship, the Nuestra Señora, I could not offer as much. But they, in turn, had their own motives for joining me . . .

The Vexilla Regis has faded.

DE MORGA. Santiago de Morga, at your service! Pilot to His Imperial Majesty, and now—Chief Pilot to the Fourth Armada. About time too. I'd sailed with three fleets to the New World. Lived there—for a year. I knew the clouds, the sudden squalls, the portents of the hurricane; the flight of birds, the smell of land; night sailing on the phosphorescent sea, in close formation, lantern light pricking the surface of the waves like fallen stars. I knew the tropics. I knew how to treat the natives, too. Stories they told—the more you beat them. And there *was* no bloody gold, except in rich men's pockets. New Granada! It was the same old Granada. I moved on, and made the sea my life . . .

Behind him a ship's boy, or 'grommet', sings as he turns the sand-clock.

GROMMET (*sings*). Sand flows
The journey goes
Watches pass
By the glass
One is gone
The second filling
Turn again
God willing
Watch the sand
And count the glasses
Soon
The long journey passes

DE MORGA. At sea you think of running home, before a gale, over white-crested water; at home all you think of is the sea. The rose of morning in the sails, a dawn breeze and the wet deck drying, and the smell of the dew. All around you white-winged ships spread out like homing birds, racing each other in the morning sun, cracking on more sail. I've been waiting for this appointment—ahh, and then Hurtado goes and brings his stargazer! His quack, his German geomancer, Alemán! If anyone can find the strait, I can! I'll *smell* it out! And he brings Alemán! Who can't get out of *bed* without using an astrolabe!

ALEMÁN *(urbane, Germanic)*. Melchior Alemán, astrologer. Author of 'Flagellus Regiomontani'—

HURTADO. Wait your turn, astrologer.

NIÑO *(basso profundo)*. Thank you. Alonso Niño. Master of the flagship Nuestra Señora del Buen Aire! We Niños of Moguer have fathers to live up to; we taught Julius Caesar how to sail. We've been to every continent—and we always return. My brothers have made their pile equipping expeditions to the New World; building ships like this one. My cousins steer them. My uncles sailed with Christopher Columbus. Have no fear, my friends! We Niños: we always return.

BERNÁLDEZ. Gerónimo Bernáldez. Master-at-arms. Marshal to the fleet. I fought beside Don Juan Hurtado at Pavia, at Algier and Azamur; at Mitrovitz and Mohacs. Where Juan Hurtado goes, I go. I brought as assistant master—

DE LA SAL. Bartolomé de la Sal.

BERNÁLDEZ. Because he does what I tell him.

HURTADO. Next in honour—

DE GÁLVEZ *(patiently)*. Tomás de Gálvez. Escríbano, or notary public. And—secretly—

OMNES. The King's agent.

DE GÁLVEZ *(over laughter, whistles)*. That's how secret it is.

Murmurs in council.

In council as we sat there safe and sumptuous, Charles turned his gaze on me . . .

Murmurs hush.

(close; to us) Blessed Lady of Guadalupe, not *me!*

CHARLES V. Suppose, gentlemen, we sold these . . . islands . . . to the King of Portugal . . . we would not wish to cause our dear brother any unpleasantness. The arrival of a Spanish fleet in the Moluccas—

THE VERY OLD GEOGRAPHER *(softly)*. The *Malucos*.

CHARLES V. In . . . waters newly Portuguese—with a warlike leader—

GRANDEE 1. *If* they arrive . . .

CHARLES V. But just in case, should we not send a man expressly to inform Hurtado of the situation—at the appropriate moment, of course?

GRANDEE 2. A spy, your Majesty?

CHARLES V. A representative. Able to keep a secret. An unobtrusive fellow . . .

DE GÁLVEZ *(to us)*. I sought to seem obtrusive.

CHARLES V. Ah yes—yes yes—de Gálvez!

De Gálvez groans quietly, as polite applause rises, and fades.

DE GÁLVEZ *(close)*. Did you forget, sweet Virgin? What about my pilgrimage? My horsehair vest? My weight in candles vowed to you? I've never been to sea! I am a Spanish gentleman. I am scared shitless.

ALEMÁN. Permit me, please? Melchior Alemán, astrologer and author of 'Flagellus Regiomontani'—a critique of certain mathematical traditions. And Navigator to the fleet. Or as my colleague Pilot de Morga, that semi-literate Basque, puts it: geomancer, stargazer, and quack. I met the strange soldier Hurtado in Vienna; we understood each other right away. There is one cause and one only, to sail west; one purpose (lost for centuries). The rest are only bullies' dreams. *This* is the journey, by Seth! (ancestor of all spiritual men, apocryphal image of Adam, and, by the by, inventor of astronomy). To find the bones. The bones of Christ. I said: we can reach the dreaded Strait by the first decanate of Sagittarius, with a Grand Trine in Fire—the aspects are to Mercury in Aries, in the House of Secrets, and in Leo, to Fortuna (the Moon's Ascendant) in the House of Dreams! The day to sail is in September: the fourteenth.

Sound of a fist slamming down on wood.

DE MORGA. *Listen* to me—

ALEMÁN. The Feast Day of the Exaltation of the Holy Cross, de Morga!
(Over his protests) 'Bring forth the cross: the standard of our King!
Shining! A mystery—whereby in life he harrowed death, by which
in death he furnished life . . .'

DE MORGA. The summer lasts four months—just four months! in
Magellan's strait. We'll freeze to death if we get there too late!

ALEMÁN. September the fourteenth. At five hours after midnight.

DE MORGA *(groans)*. Perfect. We'll miss the tide.

ALEMÁN. We'll get down the Guadalquivir, de Morga. We'll glide over
the Maine Ocean . . .
> The sea of Weedes won't make us wait,
> We'll quickly thread Magellan's strait.
> Thereafter the charts don't augur
> Quite so well, my dear de Morga,
> Not for you, at any rate . . .

DE MORGA. You stick to *your* charts, Jew. I'll stick to mine.

ALEMÁN *(polite)*. Please—*former* Jew! Or shall I call you Muleteer de
Morga? Wasn't your father—

Splintering wood, oaths, and the sound of a man being forcibly restrained.

HURTADO *(as the sounds fade)*. Alemán, de Morga: they weren't the
only ones already fighting. Half pay in advance is more than most
adventurers can handle: often you bury men before you leave. At sea
the dead and their eternal portion were to be referred to God by—

DE LA CUEVA. Fray Alejandro de la Cueva. Chaplain to the fleet.
Bishop-elect of the Island of the West. Protector of the Islanders, by
patent of the Emperor. His most Christian Majesty, greatly moved by
the prospect of new and vast Dominions for our Catholic Church,
has insisted that all voyages include a clergyman charged with preaching

the Christian message. I, padre prior, Hieronymite monk and prior of the monastery of St Jerome in Cordova, have the honour of being chosen, in recognition of my piety, my learning, my devotion to the poor and to the spreading among them of God's holy word. May Christ our Lord permit us to accomplish this voyage in His service!

OMNES. Amen!

HURTADO. I found this cleric in the Arenal; in brothel-town; his family paid me to ship him west. At the time of sailing de la Cueva was no more prior at Cordova than he was Bishop of the Indians, or their 'Protector' — he'd been removed, for venery. No congregation would abide him. Several paid him handsomely: to allow them to pursue their heresies unsupervised. The New World was a dumping ground for men like this. But de la Cueva, though abominably vain, was not wholly dislikable. No priest who'd lived for five years in a whorehouse could be altogether bad . . .

DE LA CUEVA. On this historic voyage I, as chaplain to the fleet, take for my helpmate and brother in the faith —

SIMÓN. Simón Pérez. Sixteen years old. Novice at the Hieronymite monastery, in Cordova.

DE LA CUEVA. On account of his great piety, his learning —

A woman chuckles, low, interrupting de la Cueva, who sighs.

The truth is . . . that the boy *is* pious; and remarkably learned. He is also, though he doesn't know it, my son.

HURTADO. There were two more places in the flagship afterguard, those whose rank and salary permitted them to eat in my cabin instead of on deck. They went to men who would be useful, in their differing ways — not on board ship but on arrival . . .

MÉNDEZ. Peralonso Méndez. Gentleman. You wouldn't think so, to look at me: I wear the penitential robe of one convicted by the Inquisition. Not many get off so lightly; few survive the cord, the water, and the fire. I am here — on one little condition, because I was once Hurtado's comrade-in-arms. The condition is this . . . at every landfall, whether threatened by cannibals or welcomed by chieftains, or faced by silence and the indecipherable jungle: I am the first to go ashore, swimming alone and unaccompanied. My crime before the Inquisition? Heresy of course. I put on clean linen one Friday. Yes; that's all. Friday is the Moorish Sunday. Proof—that I was a secret Mohammedan. My real crime? When my slave Tomé stole from my guests I poured burning pork fat on his flesh from the great taper, to make him confess; not knowing that Tomé, though himself a Moor, was a familiar of the Inquisition. He denounced me, in revenge. After the water torture I now know what it is, to drown and to return from death. Swimming ashore in shark-infested seas, be it to Hell itself, my lads, is nothing, beside it.

HURTADO. He might survive. More likely he'll be cooked and eaten, within full view of the ships. We couldn't spend our ammunition on mere cannibals to free a man already marked for doom, and we had plenty more of these. My last guest was an altogether more unusual passenger . . .

DON FELIPE (*an exotic accent, oriental*). My name, my dear good friends, is Don Felipe. I am no kind of officer in this fleet; rather a supernumerary, though I have a title: lengua, or interpreter. I am a gentleman, though not, as you will have guessed, a Spanish gentleman. Like my new friend Melchior, the great astrologer, I am a former member of another race. Who am I, or: who have I been? Prince Zula, my friends! Prince of Palawan; Rajah of Mactan; Sultan of Banguey, and other islands. I have—I *had*—as many titles as the Emperor. We princes of the Sulu Sea are full of borrowed dignities, learnt from the Arabs long ago. Our thriving ports are of an age with Genoa and Venice, as you Europeans so often forget. Mind you... after five years at the Emperor's court, (I came there on Magellan's caravel Victoria, accompanied by my reluctant retinue, who got the ship home while the Spaniards sickened) . . . after five years with Charles of Spain and elsewhere, five *long* years servicing Duchesses with a taste for novelty—

DUCHESSES. Ahh, Don Felipe . . .

DON FELIPE. —and even a few Dukes . . .

DUKES. Ahh, Don Felipe . . .

DON FELIPE. After so *many* Christian baptisms (one, even, in church) . . . I really shouldn't be the one to talk about 'you Europeans'. I, Don Felipe, renamed after the Emperor's own son, count myself more Spanish than the Spaniard. My clothes, my perfumes, my bows, my sneer—*hidalgo* to the smallest mannerism. So: why not remain as I am, an adoptive Castilian, for the rest of my days? Is it . . . home-sickness? Do I miss the fragrant breath of shrubs and trees? The pool beneath the waterfall? Do I tire of dusty Andalusia? . . . a chessboard under a perpetual noon: red earth, white stone, black wood, grey leaves. No sky, only light. So few things: and all of them statues. *(He sighs)* Do I not miss the scented breeze, the waving blossom, languors of incense on enchanted Palawan? The taste of clams—or fried bats, chicken-sweet, from islands in the Surigao Strait?

DUKES AND DUCHESSES. Ahhhh . . .

DON FELIPE. Not really. What provokes me is that in this flyblown land my comrades from Mactan and Banguey have died, slowly and horribly; of a European sickness. I too am already troubled by ugly growths; distressing symptoms. Another year in Spain (another round of Lords and Ladies) would be my last. Why not sail home a glorious reincarnation, splendid with jewels, descending on my mourning peoples like a God? With—in my pocket—patents from my friend Charles granting me temporal sway over all the islands of the China Seas! Long live the might of Spain! And long live me; its humble servant, friend, and ally!

HURTADO. Fool! to trust in Kings. And these were the cream of the volunteers! Was ever captain's table graced by a worse assorted bunch? The pilot and the astrologer, at one another's throats; merry Niño the master; tough Bernáldez, my lieutenant; poor terrified de Gálvez, sent to spy; the priest and his son; disgraced Méndez in his hempen robe; the native prince in ruff and lace. But they were ready to gamble their lives on the Nuestra Señora—whose longest journey, as they knew, had been to Lisbon and back. And ready to trust in me.

Distantly: bedsprings, uproar.

Fewer than a dozen of them—but it was a start. Bernáldez lured aboard a carpenter, a cooper, and a caulker, for ten thousand maravedís each;

which they spent in the Arenal, that seaside slum, in three days, like men possessed . . .

CARPENTER *(roaring)*. *How* much? In *this* pigsty? I've paid less in Valencia!

WHORE. Very well . . . *on* the bed, half a real . . .

COOPER. Since we're already on the bed, why don't we all get into it?

WHORE. On the bed, half a real. *In* the bed, a real. Each.

CAULKER. What if we bought the bed?

Laughter. They plunge in.

HURTADO. Two Portuguese signed up, braving unpopularity: old Pero Dias, barber-surgeon; and as steward his lover Lopes. Both diseased. Neither Our Lady of Loreto nor the learned men of Salamanca could relieve them of their pain, so now they sought the cure where they'd contracted the disease—among the natives of the Earthly Paradise. Italian Ercole the blacksmith, and his brother Annibale joined us, healthy enough but always squabbling. Last—and best of all—the gunner Irés. Irish Steve.

GUNNER. Estebán Irés—so they call me here! You'd never think a lad from Cork could marry a plump little señorita and settle down in Cádiz as Irish Steve, not in the days of Drake and singe-the-Spaniard's-beard-me-boys! Oh yes he could! A good gunner's worth money, and money makes a man at home, no matter where. My best pal John Pretty lives in Bristol with a Bristol lass—I still see him from time to time; and we fire cannons at each other (what it is, you see, the Dons don't care who fires their guns, so long as *they* don't have to). We still go to sea, Gunner Pretty and I, on different sides, but for the same reason. To get rich—and get away from our wives!

HURTADO. To get away; to get rich; to get women, before, and get cured, after. Didn't anyone join for the lure of untrodden wilderness, for the glory of being among the first—the first hundred, at any rate—to circumnavigate the globe? No. These were second-generation daredevils. They knew the odds, they wanted gold to spend before they sailed; like glory it was no use at the bottom of the sea. These were my officers, and being officers they got their gold. But common mariners were needed now, two hundred of them, to man the fleet and quell our enemies, and there was no gold for them, only the going rate; no more, no less.

Distant trumpets and the voice of the recruiting officer, behind Hurtado.

At my behest, the King's Recruiting Officer set up his gorgeous standard in the squares and forecourts of Seville and sounded his trumpets. I bribed him well. The enterprise depended on his efforts, even, perhaps, on ingenuity beyond the call of duty. In Seville just thirteen men, two of them partial cripples, volunteered . . .

The distant speech fading.

RECRUITING OFFICER *(to us)*. You'd have thought I was recruiting for the Grand Turk. God's teeth! Where were the unemployed? The promise of a square meal used to bring them running! In the name of God, King Charles, and a plate of Somo Sierra turnips!

A belch, replete.

SINGLE VOICE *(dry)*. Amen.

OTHER VOICES *(a few; reluctant)*. Amen . . .

RECRUITING OFFICER. Hurtado was right: something new was needed here. I went to Málaga and in the King's name hired a famous actor, one Manilius; an impressive speaker — and a learned man. Too learned, if anything . . .

Manilius — an ancient — practising: no crowd sounds.

MANILIUS. Men of Málaga! *(Aside:)* How's this? *(Rhetorical again:)* Come with me to the Isle of Dames — insula mulierum the ancients called it — whose eager young daughters of Eve run naked to the shore, their long hair falling over their shoulders . . .

RECRUITING OFFICER *(gently; he admires Manilius)*. Forgive me — but you did say 'Come with *me* . . .'? Will they believe that you, Manilius, the celebrated actor —

MANILIUS. No, of course not — no. No, I shall be disguised . . . in costume . . . heavily made up, if you insist. An old sailor. Unrecognisable! *(Old salt's voice)* Ah if I were as young as you, my lads, what wouldn't I give to return to Havilah the Golden . . . *(Breaks off)* No? You think they'll recognize the voice? In that case why not give them something from my repertoire — something appropriate . . . the pleading scene, perhaps, from 'Gamphesanta, or, The Queen of Turkestan':

> *(Contralto)* Prince! Have you forgotten
> The opulent palaces, the cool pavilions
> And the temples with their golden cupolas?
> The pastures of your youth, in the Mountains
> Of Aaf, whose ramparts of green chrysolite
> Run clear about the earth . . .?

Is something wrong? *(Drops the contralto)* Excuse me — is something wrong? Too literary for the waterfront? Not the poor Queen, then. Something for the baser instincts. *(Stentorian again)* Men of Málaga, take with you lead, tin, iron, and glass . . . return with gold! With rubies, diamonds, and pearls! With ivory and apes and peacocks, and homunculi in bottles, with the priceless youth-giving, metal-divining, bird-ensnaring roots of the Parebon tree of Ind, with —

The recruiting officer coughs.

Mm?

RECRUITING OFFICER. I think they've fallen for that sort of thing too often, and come back half dead with a parrot and a handful of nutmegs. It's too late to offer them treasure and romance —

MANILIUS. Too late? You're talking about my audience — I know their tastes!

RECRUITING OFFICER. Your audience goes to sea in imagination, my friend. We speak of real dangers.

MANILIUS. Well . . . it may need a different tack — at first.

Quayside hubbub; drums; trumpets. Manilius, topping the noise:

Men of Málaga! The King himself bids me address you! Men of Málaga! Listen to me!

DISTANT VOICE. We're listening, Manilius!

MANILIUS. My lads, the finest voice in all Spain brings the King's message to you, the fighting men of Andalusia: next month another fleet sails from Seville, bound for the Spiceries and golden Cipangu, a fleet more richly provided, more gloriously captained, mightier in weapons than any sent by Christendom before. A hundred culverins, my friends, bombards and pasamuros on each ship, a suit of mail for every man! Five hundred butts of Jérez wine, a thousand cheeses — this fleet will feed well and fight well, under Don Juan Hurtado de la Vega! Some of you served under him at Tunis. You know the man! A great soldier, by Santiago, and a pious man! But this fourth and greatest Armada, your King understands — men of Andalusia! — you do not wish to join! You are too old, too tired, too dull, too lazy, and too rich!

A mixed response to this; hubbub subsiding to listen, curious.

Though God in his wisdom has seen fit to give to Spain the seven thousand four hundred and forty islands of the China Sea (give or take one or two — Pliny was no mathematician, boys), the two hundred and eighty gilded cities of Cipangu, its fifty-five great rivers and one hundred and sixteen peoples . . . you prefer *Málaga!* So be it! Since you no longer wish to serve His Majesty at sea, the privilege — and the spoils — will be conferred on Portuguese and Genoese, men of firm faith and proven spirit! Not a Spaniard shall we take on board, not *one*, I say! But French, Flemings, Greeks, Neapolitanoes, Corfiotes, Negroes, and Malays!

Above rising protests:

To these, my friends! shall be confided the incense and the unguents of the East: delights of Araby shall meet *them* on the seas, swooning odours, breezes fresh with newborn flowers, indescribable perfume. Crammed with scented treasure, gold and precious stones and pearls, they shall set sail for Cipangu and drop anchor in the Sambation, that strange Sabbatic river, so-called since it flows only on Saturdays! Or as Nicander wrote (and Aelian), because it always flows — *except* on Saturdays! Theirs to discover which!

Growing tumult. Manilius goes on distantly, dispensing scraps of ancient wisdom. In foreground, we hear:

RECRUITING OFFICER *(close; to us:)*. If nobody was fooled, at least the old fellow's performance drew a crowd; one big enough to plant my own men in it, who began angrily to offer their services to the fleet. Others, true men, followed; and once fifty join, the curse is off. We moved on down the coast, to Sanlúcar de Barrameda; to Zahara, that academy of thieves; to Cádiz . . .

MANILIUS *(behind him; only scraps audible)*. Beyond Sambation, my boys, lies the Gravelly Sea, all gravel and sand without a drop of water, but which ebbs and flows like other seas and even throws up fish . . . beyond it lies the realm of Prester John, the home of Christian men . . . of elephants, dromedaries, camels, crocodiles . . . of metacollinarum, cametennus, tensevetes, wild asses . . . of centaurs, fauns, satyrs, pygmies, forty-ell-high giants, cyclopes . . . and wild women, nakedly and openly fornicating daughters of Eve, rushing to the shore, their long hair falling over their shoulders . . . to lead you to their tapestried caves, adorned with gems and featherwork . . .

RECRUITING OFFICER *(foreground, over this)*. . . . gathering men one by one; men and boys—for half my new recruits were little more than children. On our way through Andalusia we stopped off at the orphanages.

Quayside tumult has faded; Manilius' voice still faintly audible, fading.

There, in quiet courtyards in the shade of huge umbrella pines, Manilius had a respectful and attentive audience, at last. They sat in their blue tunics, a small forgotten tribe, while he set them dreaming with fanciful tales of stranger tribes and even more forgotten peoples ...

The boys speak with rising intensity—for they are all these tribes:

BOYS. *(All, low)* The Deforméd Folk . . .
    (Singly) Who roam the desert
            Rest in the shade of their gigantic feet
            And sleep in the cover of their huge ears
    (All, low) The Deforméd Folk . . .
    (Singly) The Psylli
            With one eye before
            And one behind

	A nation poisonous to serpents
(All hiss)	The Pssssylli!
(Singly)	The Agriophagi
	The panther-eating men
	With horns!
(All)	The Agriophagi!
(Singly)	The dog-faced men of Ind
	Who speak two words and bark the third:
(All)	The dog-*(bark!)* men of *(bark!)*
(Singly)	The Atlantes
	Who dread the sun
	And are no longer visited by dreams
(All)	The Atlantes!
(Singly)	The Nameless Ones

Very faintly: echoing, mirthless laughter.

(Singly)	Fleet-footed creatures of the rocks
	Who put away their dead amid laughter
(All)	The Nameless Ones!
(Singly)	Naked, night-travelling Troglodytes
	Who live in caves and catafuges
	Speak like bats
	And eat reptiles and crickets
(All, low)	Naked, night-travelling Troglodytes!
(Singly)	The Ichthyophagi
	Fish-eaters
	Who suffer their children to be killed
	Before their eyes
	Without a sign of anger
(All)	The Fish-eaters, without a sign of anger!
(Singly)	The Acridophagi
	The Locust-eaters!
	Rhizophagi
	Root-eaters!
	Struthophagi
	Ostrich-eaters!
	Elephantophagi

> Elephant-eaters!
> Pamphagi!
> Everything-eaters!
> *(All)*   Everything-eaters! Everything-eaters!

MANILIUS *(quiet, incantatory).* And on the shores of the Spice Islands, my boys, the Chelonophagi . . . who feed on turtles (and sometimes clams). Turtles as big as fishing smacks! These creatures overeat on land at night and then betray themselves by snoring! As for the clams . . . they sing beneath the sand, their voices low and sweet as eels . . . the song of clams beneath the sand . . .

BOYS *(softly).* The song of clams beneath the sand!

RECRUITING OFFICER. He fed them fantastic morsels, Pliny spiced with Marco Polo—how to hunt the Manticora . . .

BOYS. How To Hunt The Manticora!

MANILIUS *(blasé).* On an elephant.

BOYS. The dreaded Manticora!

MANILIUS. With its human face and pale blue eyes, and three—count 'em—three rows of teeth!

BOYS. Three rows of teeth!

MANILIUS. Big as a lion—but red! Red as cinnabar!

BOYS. As red as cinnabar!

MANILIUS. Its tail like a scorpion's, with one sting at the end, two at the root, and one in the crown of its head: missiles a foot long and thin as a thread. Fatal to all. Save elephants . . .

RECRUITING OFFICER. He promised them adventure; and astonishment. Riches he could not guarantee them. Too many ragged mariners came begging alms at every house of God. Yet even *they* talked of natural wonders—of an earthly paradise beyond the Great South Sea; jungles, deserts, sea and sky teeming with beasts from books . . .

BOYS. *(Singly)*   The Basilisk . . . the Cockatrice . . . the Hippogriff!
                    The Monster Rat! The Hydra . . . Mermaid . . .

Montygre . . .

MANILIUS. The seven—count 'em—kinds of Siren!

BOYS. Woman-fish! Woman-bird! Woman-horse!

MANILIUS (across them now). From the innumerable beasts, so Solinus says, impressed upon the constellations of the sky, the seed falls into ocean . . . mingling with the watery element to forge a multitude of monstrous forms: sea-bears, sea-goats, sea-hares, sea-spiders, sea-mice . . . (his voice fading as the boys build to a finale)

BOYS.	(Singly)	The Tityrus!
		The Sagittary!
		The Opinicus!
		The Orc!
		The Ass-Bittern!
		The Falcon-fish with a hound's ear . . .
	(All)	With a hound's ear!
	(Solo)	The Tarask . . .
	(All)	Dragon-Basilisk!
	(Solo)	The Wyvern . . .
	(All)	Dragon-man-fish!
	(Solo)	The Lamya . . .
	(All)	Woman-dragon-lion-goat-dog-horse!
		(Manilius' voice has now gone)
	(Singly)	The Minocane . . .
		Half child—
		Half spaniel!
	(All)	The Winged Satyr-fish!
		The Wonderful Pig of the Ocean!!
	(Solo)	The Wonderful Pig of the Ocean . . .

A last echoing silence.

RECRUITING OFFICER. On an ocean-going caravel, that wonderful pig of the ocean, these boys would grow up fast. And captains, I had found, were rarely sorry to see them recruited so young. They did less complaining than the old shellbacks who'd seen it all before and liked it better under Captain Such-and-such . . . the remainder of the five ship's companies I plucked out of the jails: too many for my liking —

A distant drumbeat, steady, very slow.

Thank God it was the last fleet to sail for the Isles of Spice, by that ill-fated route . . . and once the stories of their journey started reaching home, I couldn't have found twenty men to follow them, not from the prisons of the Holy Inquisition itself . . .

OMNES. HOYYY! —

A great communal shout as a sail is hoisted, and a chantey begins:

CREW. *(Solo)* O the sun . . . *(Omnes)* I say the sun!
       (Solo) Shining till . . . *(Omnes)* the day is done!

NIÑO *(background, behind the chantey)*. Haul in on the topsail sheets! Put your backs into it!

CREW. *(Solo)* When day is done . . . *(Omnes)* we make our bed!
       (Solo) And pray the rats . . . *(Omnes)* are too well fed!
       (Solo) Too well fed . . . *(Omnes)* to search for meat!
       (Solo) Too well fed . . . *(Omnes)* to gnaw our feet!

HURTADO *(as the chantey fades)*. The crew were found; by God's will; and the ships ready to sail. *(In the silence, the slow drumbeat remains, continuing)* The night before, I came aboard the flagship with my own belongings, my best glass and plate, and two companions: Yarilo the Slav, my servant, and the dog Zorya, bred from Carpathian stock and worth ten men in combat with a herd of skipping islanders. It was the Vigil of the Feast Day of the Exaltation of the Holy Cross.

A moment. Drumbeat, in the silence.

I found I could not pray. *(A moment; brokenly)* Help me, Lord! *(Silence)* Play, Yarilo . . .

In tempo with the drumbeat, a viol. The music dark, Slavonic.

(Close; to us) Suleiman was with me . . .

SULEIMAN *(close, almost whispering)*. 'Of God,' Don Juan, 'and the illimitable: God that begets not nor is begotten . . .'. The Koran. Sura twenty-two.

HURTADO. 'That begets not . . .'. And Christ?

SULEIMAN (*amused*). And Christ, Don Juan? (*A pause*) The tomb was empty. Read old Nestor. 'Past the islands of the West a Christian King lives still, and in his treasure house the bones of Christ, born of no virgin but as other men are, son of Mary wife of Joseph, and corruptible as we.' (*A moment; caressingly*) Don Juanito . . .

A ghastly sound as the bow crashes discordantly across the viol strings. Then silence, and the slow drumbeat persisting. Now waves lapping softly.

HURTADO (*more under control*). I took at midnight the modeno watch, and held a private vigil on the waistdeck. In beds brothels and confessionals, throughout Seville, two hundred men were praying . . . in one fashion or another. From the Arenal came light, and music, the chacona, the guineo, the yé-yé. Were *any* asleep? Old hands perhaps. Pilot de Morga, sailing his mattress in the dark of the moon, hearing the breakers thunder on the rocks . . .

DE MORGA. Keep her off, damn your eyes, or must I go below and take the stick myself?

HURTADO. . . . searching in dreams Magellan's strait, exploring every inlet, every bay; clawing off a lee shore, round the barren headlands. Elsewhere, no less industrious, by candlelight: his rival, the astrologer — using the last night to extract helpful particulars from almanacs too heavy to accompany him on the voyage . . .

ALEMÁN. To the orb of the progressed moon Ptolemy grants five degrees of orb; Placidus, on the other hand —

HURTADO. . . . dipping his pen into the cow's horn filled with ink. De Gálvez, making his will; Méndez too — or did he make one when the Inquisition came to fetch him? Niño and Bernáldez, dreaming conquistadores' dreams —

NIÑO. Of Mezzoramia . . .

BERNÁLDEZ. Whose groves bear fruit all the year round; whose flowers never fade; whose women never grow old . . .

NIÑO. Only one road leads to it, and the road is hard to find and easy to lose again . . .

BERNÁLDEZ. And no man ever found this secret highway—save Gaudentio de Lucca; he travelled it to its end, and lived for twenty years behind the desert's curtains in a land of every felicity . . .

HURTADO. While my native prince in his soft bed breathes:

DON FELIPE. Home!

HURTADO. In back rooms on the waterfront the officers munch love-apples with their last land-loves; counting their remaining coins: one more . . .

WHORES. I'm a ship loaded with red hot cinnamon, pregnant with pepper . . .
I'm mace . . .
I'm nutmeg—smell me . . .
Ride me, I'm the sea . . .
I'm a rat, chewing your toes at night . . .
I'm a sail, catch me . . .
I'm a jar of Illescas strawberries hidden in your best boots . . .
I'm a sea swallow, flapping on your deck . . .
I'm a quail, I've got the falling sickness, stop my fall . . .

HURTADO. While those too pious or too poor to share these revels assemble their lucky trinkets, portraits of the Virgin, rings . . .

SAILOR 1. Garnet preserves health; ruby a remedy for plague; turquoise protects from accident; jasper a febrifuge; agate prevents tempests . . .

SAILOR 2. Should I take my marked cards? What if I'm caught?

SAILOR 3. They say a King out of a deck of cards is worth eight chickens to an island chief . . .

WOMAN. Take this handkerchief . . . remember how we first met, in Segovia, under the aqueduct . . .

HURTADO. First light! And a glimpse of frightened boys, gathering on the quayside where the old men have come to wave us off, and reminisce.

OLD SALTS. Eight days we lay by for a wind . . .
   . . . his arms bursting, black blood ran down the deck . . .
   . . . never touch metal . . .
   . . . said he once ate the horn windows off the lanterns . . .
   . . . chewed the leather chafing-gear . . .
   . . . sailing to all appearance out of danger . . .
   . . . from eyes to tail a cable's length . . .
   . . . I cried How wind ye? and the Steerman . . .
   . . . maggots bred in the penguin flesh, you see, they damn near stripped
us bare of clothes . . .
   . . . and God be praised! the Saint delivered me . . .
   . . . said he once chewed the lantern horn . . .
   . . . chewed the leather chafing gear . . .
   . . . in the great heat casting our skin like serpents . . .
   . . . vanished! In Bottomless Bay!

With a sudden flourish, the drumbeat ends. Silence. Then sea birds.

HURTADO. Dawn has broken on the wide Guadalquivir; the tide, breath
of the living earth, turns, and the polished marble surface of the river
slides towards the sea. Oleanders hang fire on the river banks, awaiting
the first wind. The fleet stands, poised.

Distant oar splashes, coming closer.

Slim pinnaces, charged with the silent crew, approach, a grave flotilla.
Young Niño in the leading vessel.

NIÑO (*calls across the water*). Good morning Don Juan! A fine morning
for catching turtles. Shall we go fishing?

Hurtado chuckles.

How's that wolf-whelp of yours faring? Has she found her sealegs yet?

HURTADO. She'll find your legs, my Niño, if you're not careful with her.

Niño laughs, distantly, then mutters to the men beside him.

He makes some scurrilous joke, but no-one laughs. They are like
men going to an execution.

In background, orders, voices, armoured tumult as the boats reach the flagship.

They come aboard: officers, mariners, men-at-arms, their breast and shoulder plates and helmets shining. Last of all, the two Hieronymites in their dark scapulars. Fray Alejandro and the boy, fresh-faced. On the greatest day of his life. Your name, boy?

SIMÓN. Simón Pérez, Captain.

HURTADO. Age?

SIMÓN. Sixteen, captain.

HURTADO. Ever held mass on a swaying deck with the salt spray in your eyes?

SIMÓN. No, sir.

HURTADO. Have you learnt any songs fit for a sailor's ears, Simón?

SIMÓN. Yes.

HURTADO. Then sing one. *(Calling)* Fray Alejandro, assemble the men!

Voices, orders, as they assemble. In foreground, Simón sings:

SIMÓN. Give thanks
　　　To the light of day
　　　To Him that sends
　　　The night away
　　　And Her to Whom
　　　All sailors pray
　　　Bless the cross
　　　Glorious tree
　　　And the Lord
　　　Of Veritie
　　　And the Holy
　　　Trinitie
　　　Bless the soul
　　　Given to all
　　　That sons of Eve
　　　After the Fall
　　　May their immortal

Portion call
Give thanks!

As the assembled crew launch into the Salve Regina, we hear, foreground:

HURTADO. As we sing the Salve and the Litany of Our Lady of Loreto I look into their faces: my companions on the noblest voyage ever undertaken by Christian men. And what have they to offer? Broken fortunes, rambling dispositions; terror; greed. For the time being let them dream of pearls and pepper and terrestrial paradise. Ours will be a greater prize than gold or spice, a treasure lost, unheard of, unthought of since the dawn of faith. A very sacrament: relic of relics: the supreme testimony to the Christ who suffered in the flesh. And left us His Body. Secret of Secrets! Lost: and found again, now, to redeem our rotting church and raise it once more to the skies. Nestor! Old anchorite! My guide!

The singing ends. A silence.

Silence falls, at the elevation of the host. All eyes are turned to me, for the signal. On the Santa María La Blanca, the San Cristóbal, the San Gil, the Ysabel: decks crowded, waiting. Only one face, on the waistdeck below me, is averted: one face: young Simón, still gazing at the host raised in Fray Alejandro's hands; unflinching, at the body of Christ. His Body! One follower of Seth, then, one true knight. (*A sound of armour*) Now: I kneel; and two hundred and fifty men kneel with me, watching. (*Sounds, across the water, then silence*) Until I cross myself. And rise again.

The heavy sounds once more.

(*A shout:*) May God our Lord permit us to accomplish this voyage in his service!

OMNES. Amen!

HURTADO. Laus Deo!!

OMNES. Laus Deo!!!

Sound is unleashed, on board and on shore. On board a great cheer, echoed on shore. Cannons sound; trumpets; drums beating. Distant peals of bells from the shore. *Across the pandemonium the orders to weigh anchor, the rattle of heavy chain.*

HURTADO. Trumpets, drums, cannon; holy bells; and on the Dock of Mules a distant band, survivor of the night's revels, play us an unholy farewell. Link by link the anchors rise, invisible; breaking the surface to a tumultuous cry. At the top-gallant our colours feel for the wind. We're moving! And the spell is broken — men dance, hug, clap each other on the shoulder . . .

Shouts, whistles, stamping noises, rising in volume.

Under bare poles, our virgin sails still furled, we drift out into the river.

Rising sounds of wind and water.

(*Shouts:*) We're off to the Moluccas, boys. Voyamaluco!

CREW (*a roar*). Voyamaluco!

As the roar spreads to the other ships:

HURTADO (*close; to us*). Now by Seth the living Christ, by Seth who named the stars, thirdborn to Eve, thrice-male, immortal, incorruptible, guide us thy missionaries to Maluco, to the bones of him who died corruptible as we: prisoners of flesh and guardians of illimitable light! Voyamaluco!

OMNES. Voyamaluco! Voyamaluco!

Music rises, gradually drowning the voices and the shipboard sounds.

End of Part One.

Part Two: THE KNIGHTS OF SETH

The Knights of Seth, Part Two of The Sea Voyage, was first broadcast on BBC Radio 3 on May 16 1989. The cast was as follows:

JUAN HURTADO DE LA VEGA	Philip Voss
SIMÓN PÉREZ	John McAndrew
GERÓNIMO BERNÁLDEZ	Trevor Peacock
SANTIAGO DE MORGA	Norman Jones
MELCHIOR ALEMÁN	Struan Rodger
ALEJANDRO DE LA CUEVA	David Sinclair
ALONSO NIÑO	Joe Dunlop
TOMÁS DE GÁLVEZ	Donald Gee
PERALONSO MÉNDEZ	Christopher Good
DON FELIPE (PRINCE ZULA)	Sam Dale
IRISH STEVE	Ken Cumberledge
YZQUIERDO	David Goodge
PACHECO	Christopher Scott
TRISTÁN	Ian Targett
CHAMBERLAIN	Philip Sully
MADRE PACÍFICA	Jo Kendall
WHORES and NATIVE GIRLS	Alice Arnold, Marcia King, Joan Walker
SAND-CLOCK BOY	Clive Samways

SAILORS, ANIMALS, CRIMINALS, and other parts, were played by members of the cast.

Director: Jane Morgan

Lapping waves and, distantly, the Salve Regina, the ancient hymn sung every evening by the seaborne conquistadores. Their untrained, raucous, unaccompanied voices swell and fade, on the wind.

The hymn ends. Silence, then, at a distance, a brief flourish of trumpets, and the voices of the Master-at-arms and the Captain-General, in turn:

BERNÁLDEZ. Instructions to the fleet hereby proclaimed the Fourth Armada to the Isles of Spice, under the command of His Excellency Don Juan Hurtado de la Vega, Knight Commander of the Order of Santiago!

HURTADO. Article One! The first preoccupation of His Majesty is the spreading of our Holy Catholic Faith and the salvation of the souls of those yet unbelievers, to bring them to the knowledge of God and the love of Jesus Christ our Lord!

DE LA CUEVA *(nearer)*. Amen!

CREW *(close)*. Amen!

HURTADO. Article Two! If during the voyage to the Malucos new islands are discovered within the line of His Majesty, they shall be placed on the marine chart in writing, in their longitudes and latitudes. If the new islands are inhabited, speech should be had with the natives and a sign left to show that they were discovered by order of His Majesty. If gold or spices or other valuable products are found, some time may be allowed to trade, without abandoning the principal object of the voyage. If any religious will remain voluntarily, it may be arranged for them to land, with orders to ascertain the quality of the country and to return to the fleet if they do not wish to stay. In landing, well-known hostages should always be secured, to make sure that the ships will be safe and well supplied...

Above this distant proclamation, we hear a youthful voice, close:

SIMÓN. On the day of St Mathias, by God's grace, after eight days sailing, we arrived at the port of Gomera in the Canaries, where we took in wood and water, pitch and fish, and many fine cheeses. Having said Mass at the Church of the Assumption we sailed again the first Sunday in October, and lay by three days for a wind, on the meridian of Hierro, near to Cabo Verde. While we lay there becalmed, the Captain-General read to us His Majesty's instructions to the fleet.

NARRATOR *(same foreground acoustic)*. So begins the journal of Simón Pérez of Cordova, of which the original, or a copy of it, was unearthed in a crypt in Manila, during the spring of this year. A shortened version of Simón's journal had been rendered into English — its sources remaining a mystery — in the 17th century; this translation, some little modernized, serves our purposes here. And, thanks to the Manila find, material once omitted from it can be added again, in the author's style: he is a young priest, a Hieronymite novice of sixteen. His tone is brave — considering the misery of his first weeks at sea...

SIMÓN *(while Hurtado continues declaiming the instructions to the fleet, in the background)*. But three days out from Sanlúcar the pump failed on the Ysabel and we were obliged to put in at the isle of Porto Santo for repairing of it. I was glad of this, and on enquiring whether I might go ashore to make our business known among the townspeople, in accordance with His Majesty's commandments, I was granted permission to do so, in the company of several men-at-arms. These soon found other business, for once on land and seeing me still sea-sick they abandoned me and fell to killing of the many rabbits that inhabit the island, the men discharging their weapons so freely that no living creature was safe. At which the populace became enraged, and taking stones to my protectors chased us to the pinnace, wherein we embarked in haste and so came again to the ship before I had time to subdue my sickness, which was the true reason for my desiring to go ashore.

Behind Simón's narration we hear Hurtado continuing, raising his voice above the chatter of the crew:

HURTADO *(distantly)*. . . . Article Three! Regarding land within the line of our . . . *(Hurtado pauses; louder)* Article Three! Regarding land within the line of our beloved brother John of Portugal, on no pretext is any person in this fleet to discover or touch at land under Portuguese dominion!

BERNÁLDEZ. Except by chance.

HURTADO (*over laughter*). By chance? Why any man so much as looking upon Portuguese water . . .

SEAMAN (*close to us; mocking; as Hurtado's voice is drowned by shouts of derision*). Will be thrown to Portuguese sharks.

HURTADO. Article Four! On reaching the Malucos agreements should be made with the King of the Spice Islands and his heirs, with reference to the price of each article, and these prices should be sworn to and fixed for always. Also with regard to the prices of those articles brought to them from Spain, such as linen, copper, iron, and mercury, and vermilion, which are most valued by them there, these prices should likewise be sworn to and fixed for always . . .

NARRATOR (*close; over the above*). Since Porto Santo, where his men fell foul of the local populace, was a Portuguese possession, we can judge what Hurtado thought of His Most Christian Majesty's commandments. As for the rabbits Simón ascribes to the islands, they were doubtless descendants of the single pregnant doe left there some forty years before and whose offspring promptly ate all the new-planted crops, forcing the conquerors to retreat to nearby Madeira. There, in an attempt to clear the woodland and sow more crops the Portuguese began a fire which raged out of control for seven years. The conquistadores, it may be said, were rarely masters of the arts of peace.

2ND NARRATOR (*different tone; scornful*). The conquistadores!

3RD NARRATOR. Masters of perjury, treachery, guile, venality . . .

Wind and waves growing steadily louder, stormier; Hurtado, raising his voice above them:

HURTADO. No blasphemy, no swearing and no gaming to be permitted on this voyage. No renegades may ship with us, and no man come aboard without a true certificate of confession; should there be any such he must confess within three days or go on short rations of water till he does.

SEAMAN (*close to us; unheard by Hurtado*). Confess my arse, Don Juan.

HURTADO. For the rest, punishment at the pleasure of the Marshal of the fleet, as follows —

BERNÁLDEZ. For blasphemies! As, '*damn* so-and-so'. . .

OLD SALT (*under his breath*). Thirty days in irons . . .

BERNÁLDEZ. . . . thirty days on a first offence, for an obdurate blasphemer six months in the galleys. For 'I disbelieve . . .' or 'I curse . . .', marooning on a desert island if of genteel birth, for ordinary expedicionarios the tongue cut out and two years in the galleys . . .

OLD SALT (*along with him*). . . . in the galleys. (*Anticipating*) For gamblers . . .

BERNÁLDEZ. For gamblers —

OLD SALT. . . . the hands cut off . . .

HURTADO. And for babblers, Juan García, the tongue pierced with a burning iron.

Hoots, shouts from the crew.

(*Silencing them*) Sailing orders! Night sailing: the flagship will show two lights if the fleet is to come about or wear; three, to reduce sail; four, to . . .

Wind still rising, howling now; Hurtado's distant voice starting to fade.

. . . strike sail. Any ship from which land is sighted should fire a gun, and if at night the first that sees it shall fire two shots to leeward. If the Captain-General wishes to change tack he shall make two flashes. If . . .

2ND NARRATOR (*foreground; during the above*). The conquistadores! Seaborne leeches of every kind and quality from aristocratic swindlers to cutpurses.

3RD NARRATOR. Each one sailing with a clean sheet, the delicate of soul absolved ashore, the unashamed in crowded quarters, within everybody's earshot — as Brother Simón notes in a discreet Latin locution...

SIMÓN (*close*). *Coram nautis* I heard confession that same night . . .

Creaking timbers; farther off, the storm, and faintly, Hurtado's voice continuing with the instructions, and contending with the elements.

. . . and of the seven kinds of thievery, so God be my witness, I left not one unpardoned in His name; each trade more villainous than the last . . .

2ND NARRATOR. Capeadores!

CAPEADOR. Mantles and capes a speciality, father . . .

3RD NARRATOR. Salteadores!

2ND NARRATOR. Highwaymen . . .

SALTEADOR. Stand and deliver absolution, boy!

SALTEADORES. Or we'll salt-eador your tail . . .

3RD NARRATOR. Grummetes!

THE GRUMMETES (*together*). Ship's boys we! (*Singly*) Fast up a rope ladder . . . into an open window.

2ND NARRATOR. The so-called . . . 'apostles'. . .

THE APOSTLES (*chanting*). Like the blessed St Peter we carry a handsome bunch of key-ey-eys.

3RD NARRATOR. 'Satyrs'. . .

THE SATYRS. See our cloven hooves, father? What do you think *we* steal?

OMNES. Moo-oo!

2ND NARRATOR. Cattle thieves . . .

3RD NARRATOR. And 'devotees', who steal—

THE DEVOTEES (*pious*). Only from the *best* churches.

2ND NARRATOR. Lastly the dreaded Matones . . . who never steal.

3RD NARRATOR. Except for one item.

The Matones chuckle, low.

THE MATONES. We come to steal your life, my friend.

Distantly, Hurtado's sailing orders, battling the storm, now culminate in:

HURTADO. Article the last, of His Majesty's instructions! In the event of the death of the Captain-General, he is to be succeeded by Don Jorge de Estrada, one of the captains of the fleet, who will remain in the Spice Islands. Failing him, Rodrigo Ruiz de Trassierra, one of the captains of the fleet. Failing him . . . Hernando Rojas . . .

Crack of thunder. Hurtado's voice fades:

. . . failing him . . . Anton Coronado . . . failing him —

SEAMAN *(close)*. Failing him, every man for himself.

More thunder and a great cry as the first wave breaks over the waistdeck and the ship rolls, throwing the men below across their crowded space.

2ND NARRATOR *(as before, unpitying)*. The conquistadores! Spreading terror and disease across the globe —

3RD NARRATOR. Smallpox, hookworm, malaria . . .

2ND NARRATOR. Bringing back syphilis and spices, and the plunder that financed the Renaissance.

3RD NARRATOR. Its palaces. Its paintings.

2ND NARRATOR. While they themselves starved, drowned, died in squalid brawls: these were Simón's new flock. Their Mother Church was sick. Corrupt, exhausted, and imperilled from within. The plunder gilded her. The plunderers cared not a fig — except when peril threatened *them* . . .

Another cry, and the sound of urgent prayer, de Gálvez leading, others joining in. Shouts, orders, in background. Praying continues, foreground:

DE GÁLVEZ. Blessed Lady of Loreto save us, Holy Virgin of Guadalupe preserve us, Sweet Lady of Antigua intercede for us, Holy Mother save us . . .

NIÑO *(distantly)*. Ho, de proa! Strike the foresail!

DE MORGA *(same; calm)*. Hold fast, Steerman! West, nothing to the northward, nothing to the southward!

DE LA SAL. Make fast the boat there! Look sharp!

SIMÓN (*close; over the above*). About the hour of Compline, the sea run-ning up very high and strong, a furious wind came out of the Gulf of Guinea and drove us onto the main Ocean. We ran before it under bare poles, dry tree our sailors call it but there was not one of us dry that night, the tempest following us unabated. Of our comp-any below, many feared for their lives and wept aloud, the masts and hull groaning with them and the beasts in the hold making such moan that those of us who would have sung the Credo could not, for their noise.

Muffled cries as the ship rolls, animals bellowing, men praying.

Some confessed anew. Others, with penitential vows . . .

SEAMAN (*background*). Save us, Lady of Consolation!

MÉNDEZ. Your weight in candles, Great Queen of the Seas!

ANIMALS. Moo-oo!

SIMÓN. . . . blamed their unquiet lives, forswearing their sins and pledging, if we came safe again to Spain, to go in procession into the mountains of Estremadura . . .

DE GÁLVEZ. In my shirt, sweet Virgin!

ANIMALS. Moo-oo!

SIMÓN. . . . the rest braving the danger with greater fortitude, in calmness repeating the Rosary and the Litany of Our Lady; but all — in truth — wishing ourselves the lowest animals ashore.

OMNES. Moo-oo!!

This below-decks uproar fades, leaving the sounds of wave and wind; spray hitting the deck, and the intermittent creaks of the ship. Between these, short bursts of whispered prayer, intense and indecipherable.

SIMÓN. That night I heard confession of my Lord Bishop, and was afraid for my soul.

DE LA CUEVA (*despairing; hoarsely, weak*). Simón!

SIMÓN. In the dark of the moon I went on deck, the sea still high and our ship spooning before it, and soon what little I had eaten I vented on the wild waters, as if delivering to them all the foul deeds confided to my bosom since we left Seville. (*A moment; shuddering*) And yet not all; one I could not disgorge. In his delirium my Lord Bishop de la Cueva . . . called me his own boy and the son of his body.

We hear Simón retching.

(*Close to weeping, in his narration*) And swore to it . . .

DE LA CUEVA (*as before*). . . . on the Holy Cross! It's true, Simón. I sired you, fed you, watched over you . . .

A woman laughs quietly, caustic.

(*Interrupting her*) . . . commended you myself to the priors at Cordova. I swear it on the Cross, Simón. Stay with me now . . . hear my confession, I beg you . . .

Punctuated by the crashes of the waves and the rise and fall, in the background, of the fiercely whispered prayers, we hear Simón crying.

His own voice resumes, close, calmer but still shaken by the memory:

SIMÓN. From the lips of those who think their last hour is come, there was no blasphemy I could not credit, no vile act left unuttered; nor one among us fit to be saved; *none*. So I supposed. Yet that same hour, when I had found a father I could never honour; knowing now that I was made in sin, and fatherless for ever; that same hour . . . he saved my life. He: that *he* who was more than a father. That he who died at the hand that writes this. No: alas my reader no not Christ our Lord, who daily dies at every man's hand. No, a man of flesh and bone: he whom I killed: the Captain-General Don Juan Hurtado . . . who that night saved from death by drowning one who was to be his chaplain, and his executioner.

Wind, waves, louder now than groaning wood; as we move up on deck, with Simón. The sinister whispering recurs, comes closer:

We were shipping much sea over the bows, and making my way aft I came upon three men at the stern of the vessel, among them Yzquierdo, the bosun's mate, taking the modeno watch that night; all three in prayer, by their ardent whispering. Then the ship rolled like a barrel in a surf, lifting the poopdeck, and I perceived these were a hardier sort—to all appearances, fishing! But there was stranger yet to come, for when one withdrew his harpoon from the waves I saw attached to it a portrait of Our Lady ringed with agate stones . . .

Whispering ends; voices now, shouts over the storm, threatening:

YZQUIERDO. What make you here, boy? Come to see the devil's work?

PACHECO. Have you come to watch us founder, priest?

SIMÓN (*over this; foreground*). Observing me, the others took in what I had thought their fishing lines, on which were hung instead all manner of relics sacred to mariners and set there, as I later understood, to appease the waters and temper their fury to us.

PACHECO. One wave could wash him over, and no man the wiser...

TRISTÁN. Seize him, Yzquierdo!

SIMÓN (*background*). No! As you are Christian men!

PACHECO. Catch him!

SIMÓN (*over the struggle; continuing, foreground*). Fearing their ill demeanours I hid in the pinnace which we had hoisted aboard before the tempest broke; but they laid hands on me . . .

TRISTÁN. What, would you bite?

SIMÓN (*background*). Sweet St Jerome, help me!

YZQUIERDO. He can't help you here. The sea belongs to the devil, boy: no Spanish fleet ever returned to Spain that carried priests! Didn't ye know that?

SIMÓN. Are you heathens, to deny God's dominion—

PACHECO. Stop his mouth!

SIMÓN (*continuing over this, foreground*). . . . and would have killed me, believing that religious were the cause of all misfortune at sea.

Though I struggled, yet they brought me by force to the rail . . .

PACHECO. No man the wiser if he drown.

YZQUIERDO. Pray for us, boy!

TRISTÁN. Forgive us!

SIMÓN (*over the sounds of struggle; continuing in foreground*). . . . to cast me over into salty ocean, a Jonah with no leviathan to rescue me, only the fishes of the Great Green to devour my body.

Cries. The struggle continuing, in a tremendous storm of rain and sea.

And I had found my last end upon the waters, but that our voices reached the Captain-General's cabin.

HURTADO (*yelling, over the storm*). Bernáldez! De la Sal!

SIMÓN. Clinging to a brace from the mainyard I saw him descend on us, roaring at my tormentors as he had been a lion of Libya!

Cries, shouts, fighting.

Yet too late, for then a studding sail broke free and, striking me where I hung from the yard, loosened my grip.

We hear the crack of timber.

I fell as dreamers fall, into the darkness of the waves.

We plunge with him into the water, and the shouts, the sounds of storm and struggle, fade into an icy silence.

Out of it we hear a boy singing serenely:

SHIP'S BOY (*sings*).   Sand flows
                 The journey goes
                 Watches pass
                 By the glass
                 Seven gone
                 The eighth is filling
                 Turn again
                 God willing
                 Watch the sand

And count the glasses
Soon
The long journey passes

The sound of a shepherd's pipe, distant.

SIMÓN. It seemed I lay abed and at my feet a window open on a fragrant meadow of yellow and green, the air as soft and sweet as April in Andalusia; and from afar, the sound of pipes. In dreams I went to sea again, and fell once more into the mutinous unquiet waves, where I could scarcely breathe to gasp my last: till all at once a monstrous head appeared beside me, with streaming hair and staring eyes and red mouth panting hotly, and I woke—to find a dog's tongue at my face. A wolf's tongue rather, for this was no dog but a black wolf of Carpathia, called Zorya or 'dawn' by her master the Captain-General. The blackest dawn, so it was said, was finding her aboard with us; yet Romulus and Remus had no better nurse than I this gentle helpmeet to our captain. In his cabin was I abed, and at the window no meadow, but the Sea of Weeds in which we lay becalmed . . .

The pipe has faded. Briefly, a quill pen at work and, a little way away:

HURTADO. A hundred leagues and more we made, Simón, running before the hurricane. Today the chip log seemed more to accompany us in the gulfweed than measure our speed in leaving it behind.

SIMÓN (*foreground*). I too, becalmed, lay with my limbs as useless as a babe's and, fever-drowsy, watched Don Juan pricking the chart; writing his journal, noting down whatever that day had brought forth. With his own hand, at morning and at night, he fed me medicine...

HURTADO (*closer; gently*). Sleep, Simón.

SIMÓN. Four days, he said, I was insensible and close to death, while the tempest raged.

Voices come, a little way away:

NIÑO. The foremast on the San Gil sprung by the cap, our own yards spent, the whipstaff broken—but not a man lost, praise the Lord!

SIMÓN (*foreground*). Bernáldez our marshal-at-arms and the master Niño visited me; and other gentlemen and persons of honour, though I was yet too weak to thank them . . .

DE GÁLVEZ. A safe recovery, Father . . .

MÉNDEZ (*closer*). Here's an amulet. It saved my life in Algiers. (*Low*) It's gold inlaid with jasper . . .

ALEMÁN. Let me know your nativity, my friend. I'll have the stars attest your strength.

SIMÓN (*foreground*). Did I hear aright? Some called me Father — as I thought, in idle mockery. Once it was my eyes surely deceived me, for I opened them to behold hanging before me at the window, upside down, a face . . .

IRISH STEVE. Top o' the morning, Father.

SIMÓN. Irish Steve the gunner! Though not one brought report of my three persecutors, I could guess at their fate . . .

HURTADO (*close*). Hanged from the yard, all three. Sleep now.

SIMÓN. An end no less cruel than mine, had they succeeded; yet may Christ have mercy on their souls.

HURTADO. Sleep . . .

SIMÓN. Did I sleep? Until the fever died I could not tell whether I dreamt asleep or dreamt awake; the days passed one into another till all seemed but one endless hour at sea, mocking the turning of the glass; while like a great Dutch clock unwound the ship gave time the lie, sails at the ready yet bereft of motion; thus entranced we lay by for a wind eight days: an octave in the doldrums.

Shouts of men hauling the lead; mingling with the vile suck of the pump.

Sweet sea orisons at daybreak and the stink of the pump at the diane watch; the shouts of men hauling the lead; the music: the zumba, zarabanda, the chacona, the yé-yé . . .

We hear the pipe (as before), and little drum.

There was one, a shepherd come to sea, who played the pipes, the tambour and the tambourine, so that the very sea-mews, big as swans, flew down to hear the unaccustomed music. Watching the sea birds and telling the shape of clouds, betting on next day's weather or the number of fleas in a man's britches: these were diversions for men with nothing to do but clean the ship, and clean the gear, and trawl for fish . . .

The crew pick up the piper's tune, in tempo with the ever-sucking pump:

OMNES *(chanting).*   Nothing to do but eat and shit
                and clean the gear
                and clean the ship
       Nothing to do but man the pump
                and clean the gear
                and eat and shit
                and pump
                and pump
                and pump
                HOY!

The ship's bell is rung, twice; a sound repeated on the other ships in turn.

SIMÓN.   The Captain-General held evening Mass himself, a dry Mass lest the consecrated host be spilt; while in my bed I murmured with him. And O! the singing . . .

From afar we hear a hymn, 'O crux ave, spes unica': the five ships' companies in attempted unison, loud in their piety. And Simón:

(Close; but weak; singing)   Hail to the Cross
                        The Cross all hail
                        Thou only hope of Man!

Simón falls silent, and the hymn slowly fades.

A handbell is heard ringing, distantly at first, then coming closer.

SIMÓN.   At nightfall, the last ceremony of the day: a watchman came out at the hatch, and having rung a little bell, spoke in the saddest and most doleful voice I ever heard . . .

WATCHMAN *(approaches, intoning).* Death is certain

> And most severe
> That which, dying,
> Thou wouldst have done,
> Do now.
>
> *(Retreats, repeating the chant)* Death is certain, and most severe . . .

SAILOR *(close; murmuring in unison)*   Crabs are certain
And most severe . . .

ALEMÁN *(a little way away; low).* Death is certain enough, unless we find the strait by June . . .

Slam of a hatch: the handbell and watchman's chant pass from earshot.

OLD SALT *(low).* They say Magellan lost twenty men frozen to death.

Murmuring voices, continuing. Small sounds; dice; a hen flaps wings.

SIMÓN *(close).* The great ocean was hushed; as if at prayer; the sea the night sky and its stars our church; the ships a flock whose smallest action, seaborne, reached the ear: a yawn; a footfall; in the hold a hen finding her roost; the sound of the weeds parting slowly at the ship's prow; and the murmurs of sleepless sailors keeping all awake aboard a ship just thirteen paces long . . .

SAILOR *(murmur, behind Simón).* . . .their flesh eaten by maggots. . .

DE MORGA. That damned astrologer! Had we left earlier . . .

NIÑO. These seas are calm-cursed, friend de Morga; a more northerly crossing . . .

SIMÓN *(foreground, over this).* . . . complaining, cursing fortune. Men at sea forget their vows made when a storm is up; like women when the pain is done and their confinement over.

SAILOR. . . . and of Magellan's two hundred, Elcano brought but thirty home.

DON FELIPE. Fifty, my friend.

SAILOR. Thirty. The rest were Malays.

DON FELIPE *(trying to keep his temper).* Begging your pardon, honoured sir, I shipped with Elcano, and being here the senior sailor —

PERO DIAS. Senior? I shipped with da Gama!

LOPES *(amid competing claims)*. I with Henry the Navigator . . .

YOUNG SAILOR *(to himself)*. And I with Jason and his Argonauts.

SIMÓN *(over a rising tumult; close)*. And these were gentlemen and common sailors cribbed together: quick to rail and boast and fight.

DON FELIPE. . . . and I am no Malay but Prince of Palawan and Sultan of Banguey!

SAILOR. Sultan of Pigshit.

As Don Felipe lunges at him, hens scatter, gear crashes; shouts as both parties are restrained. Quiet a moment, muffled grunts from would-be combatants. Then a cock crows loudly in alarm; and everyone begins to laugh, dissolving the tension.

SIMÓN *(foreground)*. Safer to vilify the absent one: the Captain-General — Don Chachu, as some familiarly called him . . .

MÉNDEZ. I say the pilot knows his business.

DE GÁLVEZ. For a Basque. *(A pause)* Would I could say as much for our commander.

MÉNDEZ. Must he command the winds too? I've fought beside him, sir. The general's is no common heart; believe me.

DE GÁLVEZ *(prompt with a courtly pun)*. Hart or doe; a most *un*common mariner . . .

SAILOR 2. They say his father was a pastry-cook.

SAILOR 3. If he had one.

SAILOR 4. And his mother a Jewess.

SAILOR 5. If he had one. He is immortal, surely, for he calls himself after Seth in the bible, who lived 900 years and more . . .

OLD SALT. Don Chachu is the Devil's man, that's certain. I saw him quell the storm with words of exorcism; and they came from no gospel.

YOUNG SAILOR. I heard them too!

A hubbub rises; rising within it, a viol strikes up a dark Slavonic tune.

SIMÓN *(foreground)*. To keep such talk from Juan Hurtado's ears, his servant Yarilo would fetch his viol and play; for Yarilo could say nothing in his master's defence: his tongue had been cut from his mouth while he was prisoner at Tunis.

SAILOR 2. I saw Don Chachu come aboard the night before we sailed, and with him a black goat, they say to drink its blood . . .

SAILOR 3 *(scornful)*. It was no goat—

SAILOR 4. And in a leathern cask he has the head of a Turkish adversary, preserved in vinegar . . .

The voices fade behind the viol, which remains, subdued.

SIMÓN. Yet some spoke true: for the captain had such a cask, a leather cask; and one night when my fever had abated, I saw him open it. From it he took—a heron's feather, which he kissed; and then: a book; this too he kissed; and seeing me awake . . .

HURTADO. I had these of Suleiman himself, when I was held for ransom at the fortress of Mitrovitz. *(A moment; amused)* Don't you believe me, boy?

SIMÓN *(astounded)*. You stole them from the Grand Turk?

HURTADO. Stole them? No; a gift from his own hand.

SIMÓN. Bringing the book, he sat beside me.

HURTADO. The Fourth Tractate of Seth Ante-Diluvian. Did you hear tell of it at Cordova?

SIMÓN. I shook my head.

HURTADO. Tell me, Simón. Do you believe in the resurrection of the flesh?

SIMÓN. I do.

HURTADO. Of this poor flesh? *(A moment)* When will it be?

SIMÓN. When we are dead, my lord . . . and gathered to His bosom, at the Last Judgement . . .

HURTADO. How will you know that you are dead?

SIMÓN (*pausing*). It was the strangest catechism. I could not answer him.

HURTADO. Tell me this: by what token shall we know ourselves, living or dead? Are we not dead men now? Do you know why, when Jesus rose again, not one of his disciples recognized him till he said: I am the Christ? (*A pause*) Be patient; you shall learn. I say again: are not all here dead? What is Spain, what is our Mother Church but a waterless, dead canal; its ministers locked in corruption of the flesh; insensible in spirit; deaf to the Word and blind to the source of light? *This* is the resurrection: that you can rise now, in the flesh; yes; from the dead man that you are, and know the light of Sophia, mother of wisdom and progenitrix of Christ eternal.

SIMÓN (*a beat; finding his voice*). Is this not heresy?

HURTADO (*mildly*). What heresy is it?

SIMÓN. My lord? (*Hesitating*) Why then . . . do you not blaspheme against the Church — and worse —

HURTADO. I am the Church. As you are. As are all men, when they have learnt knowledge of me; of that which the anchorites of old kept secret in the desert: the true faith, known to us by way of certain Templars, who taught that the mortal Christ was born of Mary wife of Joseph, in the same fashion as other men —

SIMÓN. My lord, the Turk speaks so!

HURTADO. Wisely.

SIMÓN. Are we not enemies of the sect of Mahomet? And of all such idolatries?

HURTADO. Simón: there is a God greater than God, and higher than the demiurge, the blind creator Samael; look at his work, this world; its chaos and its pain; and think: surely that Higher Power is pure wisdom and pure spirit — the All, Ineffable and Unbegotten One of

Origin: it *must* be so. Can this poor rotting substance be His work? This flesh? No; but of His immortal realm there is a spark in each of us; of which the Serpent knew when She and the enlightened Eve gave eyes to foolish Adam — who in his arrogance did curse the woman and the snake.

SIMÓN. Now I was sore afraid; for these were doctrines of perdition.

HURTADO. This that I tell you of was handed down by many; true and pious Christians; though not of the spiritual seed of Peter, that furious man; our guide is gentle Mary Magdalen, Christ's true disciple.

A moment. The viol has faded.

SIMÓN. These are matters more fit for my Lord Bishop's ear; I am too little schooled . . .

HURTADO. Not so. And de la Cueva . . . is aboard the San Gil. *(Hesitating)* He too is sick, Simón.

SIMÓN. Sick? How? He was afflicted by the storm; but is surely recovered —

HURTADO. It is an old sickness, one that he brought to sea with him. Contracted from women. *(Pause)* Saint Job himself suffered from it. We had no room for the bedridden here on this ship; and he is dying.

SIMÓN. I tried to speak; and could not.

HURTADO. Prepare yourself to be Father to the fleet. And chaplain and confessor to him who by the grace of God: shall restore our Church to glory.

Thunder of guns; as the San Gil's cannon fire a salvo. Then, afar off, the words of a burial service.

I have it written here in Nestor's hand that to the east of paradise and worshipped in a realm of Christian men some call Nestorians, lie the bones of Christ; awaiting us; His body, proof that he too suffered the corruption of the flesh, and became light once more; as we all may, Simón. Living, we are only men: so long as we ignore the God within.

A hymn begins, distantly, spreading to the other ships.

Tell no-one; think upon my words, and I will show you what old Nestor wrote concerning the body of Christ brought from Jerusalem by his forefathers; denied by Rome, proclaimed heretical . . . yet in our hands lies Rome's salvation. *(A moment)* And all men's. We are light and dust, as Christ was. And as he was once, so we are now. Each of us is the living Christ, Simón.

We hear a solo voice, a ship's boy who carries the hymn's final verses.

SIMÓN *(after a time; close)*. On the Vigil of the Conception of the Blessed Virgin, while we lay calm-confounded, my father the Lord Bishop de la Cueva died and was buried at sea. I saw across the waters as his body fell from the San Gil into the weeds and sank from sight; and even then I mourned with my lips, not with my heart, for I had scarcely known him as a father. That day my spirit was dizzy, and my mind incensed with all the thoughts the Captain-General had put in it. O, I was in peril then; bitten by the mad dog Hurtado; now flushed with dreams, now trembling, now penitent, believing I might lose my wits at any instant . . . for how could the bones of Christ await us here on earth? Yet—if He vanished from the tomb as the faithful reported... what then? Was His body in heaven? Surely there it was superfluous. As surely too: He *had* a body when he lived. Was he not God *and* man?

HURTADO *(close)*. Both: man and God; but never both at once, Simón. Ildabaoth the lord of matter whom we Sethians know as Samael, and sometimes called Christos, united with Sophia and descended into Jesus at his Jordan baptism; leaving Him when He died on the Cross and forsook His material body to gain another made of aether. Thenceforward he consisted of soul and spirit only: which was the cause that the disciples did not know him after the resurrection . . .

The hymn has ended. A distant voice intones briefly.

SIMÓN *(foreground)*. Were these not devils that he spoke of? Yet *was* not the flesh the devil's? Mine; my father's? The weeds had joined again where my Lord Bishop's body parted them. I tried to think of the good priors in Cordova—praying for me . . .

The distant voice ceases; a bell is rung for silent prayer.

That day the mist had lifted early, and the sky was clear to the horizon. Above us ranged the great cloud masses of Castile — *(collecting himself)* — and yet not so . . . we were at sea; adrift.

In the silence a sail flaps, once.

It was about the hour of tierce; and of a sudden the wind came east. All felt it at the same instant; heads turning — soldiers rising to their feet —

Shouts, spreading from ship to ship.

. . . rushing now to drink it at their ship's stern, as it had been wine in the desert!

The cries resound.

The sails too drank and filled to bursting . . .

HURTADO *(distant)*. Steerman! West, nothing to the north, nothing to the south!

The order is echoed on the other ships, amid a clamour of activity.

SIMÓN *(over it)*. Our spell was broken; each ship cracking on more sail to race her sisters. We were bound once more for distant ports; for tropic shores; for colder shores and for the dreadful strait into another ocean. And beyond it, east of paradise: the bones of Christ.

Cries, clamour, chanteys slowly fade, leaving only the blustering wind.

Out of this a rising sound of drums, a steady tattoo; then a final flourish, and the sound of heavy chain uncoiling.

HURTADO *(over this)*. Today, the thirteenth of December, which is St Lucy's day, we entered Vera Cruz in our finest array, drums beating and colours flying, at our main truck the imperial ensign. By God's grace we are come safe to New Spain; here to rest and take in fresh supplies. Once having said a thanksgiving Mass we dropped the great anchor our sailors call La Esperanza, and went ashore. Since I had till now no opportunity to test my skill with it, I made all speed to try the astrolabe . . .

The sounds have faded. A bed creaks.

The others dispersing . . .

BERNÁLDEZ (*gruff*). . . . to try the populace.

WHORE (*promptly, laconic*). On the bed, half a réal. In the bed, a réal. Each.

BERNÁLDEZ (*scandalized*). How much?

NIÑO. In *this* pigsty?

IRISH STEVE. I paid less in Valencia!

WHORE. This is the New World, dear. I charged less in Valencia.

Bed creaks. Grumbling, laughing, they debate what, how, and who first.

HURTADO (*over this*). Our chiefest joy is fresh water to drink and wash the caked salt from our bodies. Even Zorya delights to wallow in the clear cool rivers; and there we lie hours on end, scraping our backs against the pebbles. Huge trees descend to the shore as at Thessalian Tempe, feeding our eyes with verdure at a season when our old al-Andalus is parched and brown . . .

Brothel voices have faded.

Of the flagship afterguard only two held aloof and stayed aboard: Don Felipe our blackamoor, aggrieved that his fellows will not call him Prince, as we draw nearer to his native islands; some indeed call him Don Carlos for the way he apes His Christian Majesty; and Alemán, my faithful astrologer, who must remain—

ALEMÁN. —by order of his *most* Christian Majesty. At his special dispensation a converted Jew may look upon the New World; but not land there; lest I infect it with involuntary Hebraism.

DON FELIPE. Then I shall keep you company, my friend.

ALEMÁN. Most kind, Prince.

DON FELIPE. You call us Prince; they spit and call us Malay, blackamoor. You they call quacksalver, saltimbanco, Jew. (*Graciously*) To us you are our friend Don Melchior.

ALEMÁN (*gently; but not greatly flattered*). Thank you.

A moment. Dockside revelry can be heard, in the distance.

DON FELIPE. You play dice?

ALEMÁN. Never.

DON FELIPE. Ah.

A pause. Among the sounds of dockside revelry, a New World band.

DON FELIPE. You like to dance?

ALEMÁN. No.

DON FELIPE (*undeterred*). I learn some excellent dances in Spain. Most of all from my good friend the Duke of the Asturias. A good fellow. (*Intimately*) I made casi-casi with him.

ALEMÁN (*uneasy*). Ah.

DON FELIPE (*laughing*). It is not what you think . . . casi-casi is the blood brothership of the Rajahs of the Sulu Sea. (*A moment*) I will make casi-casi with you, Don Melchior, my friend.

ALEMÁN. Another time, perhaps.

DON FELIPE. You have work to do, perhaps? And I disturb you.

ALEMÁN. No. (*A moment; then close, to us; different tone*) It was the stars disturbed me.

The dockside music has faded. Now a rising throb of wind and waves.

At Candlemas Saturn and Mars conjunct in Sagittarius, which Paracelsus calls an evil aspect; while Posidonius the Syrian and Roman Porphyry . . .

HURTADO (*interrupts*). We'll find the strait by Candlemas.

SIMÓN. But we did not. Six weeks we laboured against wintry seas and head winds, while fog hid the jungle and our hands grew stiff from hauling in the lead. Beyond the River Plate the wind was down; we shortened sail and, on the day of St Dorothy, three days after Candlemas, dropped anchor in a bay named Juan Serrano by our captain; after the pilot of Seville who, sailing with Magellan, found the strait we hoped to find again; yet many thought it an ill-fated name, for he was one who fell beside Magellan.

Wind fading, waves less furious. Over them the thunder of ship's cannon; then a concerted cheer.

(*Over this*) Here we made our first encounter with the natives of that region, who came out to us in warlike fashion in a hundred little canoes. We ordered our cannon to be discharged, whereupon they plunged into the water like so many frogs from off a bank. It was a good anchorage and our captain being minded to maintain it, bade Peralonso Méndez swim ashore, to parley with their chiefs...

MÉNDEZ (*under his breath*). May the saints preserve me; be with me now, our Lady of Antigua, and you, virgin of Guadalupe . . .

A further cheer as he dives in. Shouts of encouragement.

SIMÓN (*continuing over this*). . . . he being a degradado or convicted man, released from sentence by the Holy Inquisition on penalty of suchlike duties with the fleet.

A moment. Isolated shouts.

I prayed to St Jerome the patron of my order; and God be praised, the saint delivered him. For they received him graciously, storm-tossed and miserable as he was; his teeth chattering so . . .

MÉNDEZ (*dripping, gasping*). . . . that I could barely speak to make my peaceful message plain to them.

A great cheer from the ship; then a hymn from all throats, a little raggedly but with playful support from pipe and drum . . .

OMNES. Bring forth the standard of our King!
        Shine forth the mystery of His Cross,
        By which in life He harrowed death,
        By which in death He furnished life!

SIMÓN (*over this, foreground*). The Captain-General then went ashore and staged a full taking-possession in His Majesty's name, along with Bernáldez the marshal-at-arms and his men, and the notary public de

Gálvez, the King's emissary . . .

Above the hymn, mocking whistles.

. . . old Cacafuego, shitfire as the men called him on account of his fearfulness. When we had sung the Te Deum and the Vexilla Regis, I too, seeing that we were met with gifts and gentle looks, went ashore to study how such men might be converted to our Holy Faith; which was the harder since they went about naked as they were born and with no more embarrassment than wild beasts; and when they requested of us that we shed our clothes, to see if we were everywhere of the human kind, some of our company were ready to oblige.

The Vexilla Regis fades. Waves, soft.

In the background a sailor patiently teaches a girl the word 'vinegar'.

The more contentious among them had fled into the jungle; those who remained were willing to assist us in finding fresh water, and even in cleaning of the ships. All save the little Ysabel in which we were to put to sea to search more nimbly for the strait, were brought to shore, hove down, careened and graved, for they were shredded by the broma, a worm that abounds in the torrid zone; their bilges scraped of ordure and sprinkled with vinegar, a task displeasing even to the hardened sailor.

NATIVE GIRLS. Vinegar! Vinegar!! Vinegar!!!

SAILOR. Good.

Wind rising now; waves stronger.

SIMÓN. With their instruction in the Holy Faith I made but little progress, and the Captain-General bade me accompany him on the Ysabel; for which I later had good reason to be thankful . . .

Distantly, over the wind, we hear the shouts of Steerman and Pilot: 'How wind ye? Keep her off, damn you . . . loosen the tacks, or we are lost! Haul on that buntline . . . put your backs into it!'

HURTADO (*foreground*). On the fourteenth of February we set the compass south to Cape Blanco, and in thirty days have made near seven hundred leagues, by dead reckoning; when last I saw the sun I took it in 54°20′; now the sky is low and grey, the wind and the waters so cold even the sea crows and other pelagic birds have left us.

Mingling with the other distant cries, a voice, sounding at intervals: '30 fathoms . . . 25 . . . 20 . . . 25 fathoms . . .'.

Since we passed the cape called Deseado, the Desired, we explore each inlet, until shallows force us back to sea, despairing of the strait. Provisions meagre now; in place of some, before departing Juan Serrano, we took on stones for ballast; wisely, for here the winds are full of treachery, and more than once, sailing to all appearance out of danger, turbulent gusts near dragged us in onto the rocks. By night forced to lie to with anchors to the north and south; hearing the breakers thunder; by day clawing off a lee shore, around the barren headlands; scudding before the wind into another inlet, false, inviting; and another, and another . . .

The cries and soundings fade. Now only the stormy wind and waves.

SIMÓN. With but a span remaining in the water jars, we were close to abandoning our search; and that gladly, our sailors being full of dire tales and superstition. That great rock which guards the strait they held for a mountain of lodestone . . .

SAILOR 1. The magnet-rock that draws all iron bolts from ships that pass it . . .

SAILOR 2. Seventeen foundered there till now, with all hands lost...

SAILOR 3. Vanished, in Bottomless Bay!

SAILOR 4. . . . the whirlpool at the end of the world!

ALEMÁN. Turn back, Don Juan! Saturn portends catastrophe!

DE MORGA. One more day! *One*, Excellency!

Over the wind, a single bird cry.

SIMÓN. It was the vigil of St Lazarus; in the first faint grey dawn, pilot de Morga, stationed in the forechains of the Ysabel, beheld a black cone pricking up into the dome of paling stars . . .

DE MORGA (*yelling, distant*). The rock! Mine the reward! The rock!

Then the thunder of the Ysabel's cannon.

HURTADO (*close*). Thanks be to Christ our Lord; for lo . . . it was the strait.

Rising tumult of cries; guns still firing.

Marking its entry, the rock on its high promontory; that Magellan called the Cape of the Eleven Thousand Virgins.

Amid the cannon and cries of jubilation, we hear the sailors, gleeful now:

SAILOR 1. Come off it . . .

SAILOR 2. We haven't found *one*.

SAILOR 3. I re-name this place the Cape of the Eleven Thousand Trollops!

SAILOR 4. And one virgin: Fray Simón of Cordova!

A cheer goes up. Behind Simón's voice the rejoicing, guns, wind and waves, all slowly fade.

SIMÓN. We fell to dancing, though we slipped like drunkards on the icy deck; all but Don Melchior; we mocked him and his stars. Yet for the great catastrophe he feared we had not long to wait.

Wind and waves return, less stormy now; benign. The sound of drums, triumphant; orderly music; now and then a musket shot.

The winds we once had battled, making south, now drove us swiftly back to Juan Serrano, and we rounded the headland with musket and drum proclaiming loud our joyful news . . .

We hear the muskets gradually fall silent, and the music break off. The drums hesitate, stutter and cease in mid-tattoo. A pause. Only the waves, lapping softly; no wind. In the silence, distantly, the wail of a starving cat.

But O the sight of our once-happy settlement, that miniature dominion better fitted to the Golden Age than to the ways of conqueror and conquered; a Hesperides; a very Eden; now turned hellish as the fiery plain of Sodom: four fine ships, dismasted, deckless, merely carcasses, lay burned along the shore as they had been charred skeletons;

the human dead beside them; and the waters brown and stained with blood where other corpses floated, beside blackened, empty casks. No living man at all, native or Spaniard; all dead, the rest vanished. All desolate, all still; so quiet that across the bay there was no sound save one lamenting cry: the ship's cat from the San Cristóbal, Black George, clung complaining to a wooden spar, adrift a cable's length from where we lay; every man silent as if stupefied, for we could scarcely credit our senses; till at last all took off their caps, and wept.

We hear Yarilo's viol sound a Slavic dirge.

HURTADO *(over this, after a moment; grim)*. Yesterday, our muskets at the ready, we set forth into the hinter regions of this wilderness. The jungle came so thick, the insects feeding on our hands and faces, that even with the aid of axes we covered no more in one day than an hour's march in open country; found no trace of our missing fellows nor of their assailants; and for our pains returned each whipped and as bloody as the most ardent flagellant. Today, the vigil of St Mark, we buried eighty more; the last; and quelled our mutineers.

The viol lament ends with a dark flourish. We hear the clink of cutlery on crockery; wine being poured; now and then the ship creaks; soft waves, distant; no voices. Hurtado, close:

One I could have killed myself; but that Gerónimo Bernáldez stayed my hand.

A moment. Clink of glass.

DE GÁLVEZ. Don Juan: with one small ship; few arms, and scant provisions save what landfall may afford; the men disheartened; and our expedition blasted at the root: take thought: we *must* return to Spain.

A chair scrapes as Hurtado rises; and is restrained. A moment.

HURTADO *(controlled rage; low)*. What man disheartened? *(A pause)* If he be of noble birth, de Gálvez, he shall be marooned and left ashore according to His Majesty's instructions; if base, the quicker death therein prescribed. *(A pause)* We have found the strait. There are those among you who know our holy mission; the rest shall learn of it. Who stays with me now stays as a Knight of Seth: for I am

Master of that great Order born of the Knights Templar. I shall instruct you. Fear not, but trust in your reward — in this world and in the hereafter, if you do the work of Seth. *(A moment)* Who would leave, leaves now.

A silence.

Bernáldez; Alemán; and you the blackamoor: I know you will not fail me. *(A moment)* Alonso Niño: speak.

NIÑO. No man can ride more than one horse at once, Don Juan; no master more than one ship; I am content.

HURTADO. Peralonso Méndez?

MÉNDEZ. I am yours, my lord. Better to die at sea, or on a strange shore, than in a prison.

HURTADO. Santiago de Morga?

DE MORGA. I found the strait. Who will believe me — unless I find the further ocean too?

HURTADO. Fray Simón?

SIMÓN *(hesitates; then, low)*. I am yours also. May God grant us his blessing.

OMNES *(except de Gálvez)*. Amen.

A moment.

HURTADO. Tomás de Gálvez?

DE GÁLVEZ *(conceding)*. Amen.

BERNÁLDEZ *(sighs; quietly)*. Praise be to God . . .

The cabin sounds fade. Wind and waves rising now, to their earlier stormy pitch. Behind Simón's voice, a chantey; same tune as previously, 'O the sun . . .'. Now grim:

CREW. *(Solo)* O the strait . . . *(Omnes)* I sing the strait!
     (Solo) Narrow as . . . *(Omnes)* St Peter's gate!
     (Solo) A gunshot wide . . . *(Omnes)* a gunshot deep!

(Solo) Pray the watch . . . (Omnes) don't fall asleep!
(Solo) Fall asleep . . . (Omnes) and run aground!
(Solo) Fall asleep . . . (Omnes) and wake up drowned!
(Solo) Fall asleep . . . (Omnes) and dream of Spain!
(Omnes) Watchman HOYY! (Solo) Once again . . .
(Solo) O the strait . . . (Omnes) I sing the strait!
(Solo) I sailed it, boys . . . (Omnes) in '28 . . .

SIMÓN (close). Of our passage through that melancholy strait the chiefest memory is of the beast Zorya, whom till then I had thought as
dumb as tongueless Yarilo; who so behowled the skies that it echoed
back off the rocky promontories, as it had been our own mourning;
for we were still stricken and numb with grief. It was a most terrible
sound; and thinking the cause of her howling was Black George, some
sailors took the unfortunate cat and threw it overboard; but still Zorya
howled; and no man dared offend the Captain-General by speaking of
it. He kept his counsel; we ours, for we had much to do; anchored,
we hunted fox and seal, and made a stock of penguin meat, the which
haunted us after, maggots relishing it better than we; afloat, we hauled
the lead and watched for rocks beneath the water's surface, till our
hands and eyes gave out. We saw no fires on the southward bank,
that shore named the Tierra del Fuego by Magellan, nor any other
sign of habitation, and were the more astonished when one day about
the hour of prime we spied a man in Spanish clothes, tanned like a
native yet a European by his looks and bearing, kneeling at the water's
edge; he waved to us, as we had been an ox-cart passing on the road
to Cordova; and turned back to his business. Thinking him a survivor
of Loaysa's vanished fleet, we put to shore in haste, but seeing us
approach he grew distracted, and fled; and we saw him no more.

*Behind Simón the chantey has faded; in the silence now, above the milder
wind and waves, we hear Zorya's wolf-howls, echoing.*

*The howls fade. Rising in their place, the shepherd's merry pipe and drum,
the sounds of dancing, cheerful hubbub. No wind.*

HURTADO (close). We debouched this day, rejoicing, onto a calm and
spacious water; and being sailors, danced; for we had left behind the
Ocean Sea, that fretful sea, and were come at last to the Pacific.

SAILOR. El mar pacífico . . .

ALEMÁN. The Great Green!

NIÑO. Sweet sea of islands; and odoriferous breezes.

DON FELIPE *(softly)*. Home!

As the sounds of pipe and dancing fades, we hear a hymn, very distantly.

SIMÓN *(foreground)*. At evening the departing sun, tracing fine shadows on the water, lit a pathway to the Island of the West; and we sang the Salve to a sea of beaten gold.

SAILOR 2. El mar pacífico!

DE MORGA. A woman, my friends! The other a brawling ruffian.

BERNÁLDEZ. A fine, welcoming woman.

MÉNDEZ. Thanks be to Mary, Mother of God: la madre pacífica.

SIMÓN. Speaking to us —

MADRE PACÍFICA. . . . of gentle breezes; swooning odours; sweet the scented treasure of the Islands of the West: within your grasp. Rest now.

The hymn has faded. Silence.

SIMÓN. We rested; sailing north along the coast until we found a pleasant anchorage, the forests there with game abounding, and unpeopled, undisturbed save by our sport; where we made all ready to put to sea once more, thinking ourselves restored by fortune; yet our troubles had scarce begun.

Rising, in an indoor acoustic — strange and claustrophobic now — the hubbub of the Spanish court, in a hall echoing with whispers, close to us, and low voices.

Three blows on a marble floor, with a heavy staff. Voices, whispers continue, ignoring the chamberlain's proclamation.

CHAMBERLAIN *(some way away)*. By Order of His Imperial Majesty King Charles, as published in Saragossa on the fourteenth day of April, are ceded to John, King of Portugal, all rights and titles prerogative to those our islands called Moluccas or Maluchoes . . . *(his voice fading)* . . . voiding all treaties entered into heretofore by the inhabitants of said Moluccas or Maluchoes . . .

Voices, whispers and proclamation fading. In their place soft waves and now and then creaks from the Ysabel at anchor. Close, a quill pen writing on parchment.

A knock at the door, several times, firm. Closer, Zorya growls.

HURTADO. Hush, Zorya. Yarilo . . . see who knocks.

He continues writing; the door is opened and a man steps in; door closes.

DE GÁLVEZ. Good day, Don Juan.

HURTADO *(still writing)*. The best of days.

He signs, with a final flourish.

Well, sir? *(A moment)* Be seated.

DE GÁLVEZ. Our business is His Majesty's, and private. His instructions, given me before we sailed.

HURTADO *(amused)*. De Gálvez: there is none aboard more private than Yarilo.

DE GÁLVEZ. He needs no tongue to write things down.

HURTADO. He neither reads nor writes. Now, since you will not sit with us: your business?

DE GÁLVEZ. Sealed up in wax; but you may open it.

Whispers of a scroll, deposited on a table.

HURTADO *(picks it up, examines it)*. Not yet, I think. *(Reading)* To be entrusted to the Captain-General on the last day in April, in the year of our redemption 1529. Twelve months hence. Thank you; I'll open it on the appointed day.

DE GÁLVEZ. Read it now. If not I'll tell you what it says.

HURTADO. The Spiceries are sold; and our voyage a stalking horse to raise their price.

A moment; de Gálvez dumbfounded.

DE GÁLVEZ. If you knew this, why did we risk the strait? Why sail on now, our duty done, into waters no longer ours?

HURTADO *(pauses).* Come ashore with us tonight, de Gálvez; you shall have your answer.

The sound of crickets replaces the cabin acoustic; footfalls; an owl hoots. Rising behind Simón's voice: whispers, low voices.

SIMÓN. While we lay anchored off Cape Providence, so designated by our Captain, we were admitted to the Order of the Knights of Seth; to this end, under the guidance of Bernáldez and Don Melchior Alemán, who were already of the brotherhood, the marshal's men-at-arms had made a shelter in a wood close by, fashioned of rough-hewn stone, adorned with antlers, featherwork, and other of our forest spoils; where they might practise their observances and, at nightfall, administer the rites.

The whispers, indistinct at first, multiply behind Simón's narration, across each other like a round or fugue, repeating:

1ST VOICE. Who is there?

2ND VOICE. An earthly body; holding the spiritual one imprisoned in ignorance . . .

3RD VOICE. What is to be done with him?

4TH VOICE. Kill his body; and purify his spirit . . .

5TH VOICE. Then bring him to the place of justice.

SIMÓN *(foreground, over the whispers).* The manner of it was in this sort: on the eve of our departure, an hour before the Angelus, we came ashore, and our hands being first bound, our eyes bandaged and a cord placed around our necks, we were led one by one into the wood, and on reaching the door whereof Bernáldez was the keeper, the Captain-General knocked nine times until he opened; then must the hierophant or seeker after wisdom answer as instructed . . .

We hear the nine knocks; then:

BERNÁLDEZ. Who is there?

SIMÓN. An earthly body; holding the spiritual one imprisoned in ignorance . . .

BERNÁLDEZ. What is to be done with him?

HURTADO. Kill his body; and purify his spirit . . .

BERNÁLDEZ. Then bring him to the place of justice.

Two short, ominous drum rolls are heard, ending with a flourish; then Yarilo's viol.

SIMÓN (*foreground, over the viol*). When at last we were unbound and the bandage removed from our eyes, we saw, set upon a table, a lighted candle, an ink-horn, pen, paper and sealing wax. Beside them two red cords, a naked sword, a bowl of water; and a book, which was the Book or Testament of Nestor. From this was read to us of Christ his bones conveyed in secret from Jerusalem; and from another text, the Paraphrase of Seth our founder.

HURTADO (*a little way away*). Great Seth, third son of Eve, image of God, whom the Mother brought into the world to replace the baser seed of Cain and Abel; causing the Flood to wipe them out; thrice-male Seth, made incorruptible and present through the ages until his mission is done, for as foretold in the Gospel of the Egyptians, a conflagration will come upon the earth, and grace will be with those who belong to his seed; Seth the scribe, who with the knowledge of Egyptian Thoth devised the alphabet; whose seven books were laid on Ararat to survive the flood; the Three Pillars, the Paraphrase, the Tractates and Apocalypse of Seth; who learnt the future, in hieroglyphs discoursing with the angels, and returned to earth pneumatic and invisible, newborn of the divine breath...

Hurtado, Bernáldez, and Alemán, in unison:

INITIATES. Our avatar and ancestor, Great Seth the living Christ!

SIMÓN (*foreground*). The Captain-General then investing us with the title of the Order, the seal, the password and the sign, we knelt and took an oath, swearing —

OMNES. By Seth who named the stars; ancestor of all spiritual men; bearer of the divine seed; heir of Adam, and image of God!

INITIATES. Amen!

A moment. The viol music has ceased.

HURTADO. Lord, your creation yearns to be at one with you; matter yearning for Spirit; the one for the All; the self for the Other; the named for the Nameless; the name for the Unnameable; shadow for Light; and Light itself for the Source of Light. In the name of Seth your servant, grant us knowledge of the light within us, yearning for that Source.

OMNES. Amen!

HURTADO *(voice raised; invoking)*. Iao; Sabaoth; Adonai; Eloi; and you genii of fire and water Ouraios and Astaphaios, guide me now!

Silence; and after a moment the hiss of burning steel in water.

SIMÓN. Then he held the sword over the candle flame; cooled the tip of it in water; and over each of us made the sign of the Cross.

A moment.

HURTADO *(loud)*. Whom I baptize . . . will never taste death.

At once, fierce in its discords, a choral outcry: the hymn of paradise.

End of Part Two.

Part Three: CANDIGAR

Candigar, Part Three of *The Sea Voyage*, was first broadcast on BBC Radio 3 on May 23 1989. The cast was as follows:

JUAN HURTADO DE LA VEGA	Philip Voss
SIMÓN PÉREZ	John McAndrew
GERÓNIMO BERNÁLDEZ	Trevor Peacock
SANTIAGO DE MORGA	Norman Jones
MELCHIOR ALEMÁN	Struan Rodger
ALEJANDRO DE LA CUEVA	David Sinclair
ALONSO NIÑO	Joe Dunlop
TOMÁS DE GÁLVEZ	Donald Gee
PERALONSO MÉNDEZ	Christopher Good
DON FELIPE (PRINCE ZULA)	Sam Dale
SAINT JEROME	Michael Graham Cox
SULTAN	Richard Tate
LEVIATHAN	Christopher Scott
COOPER	Ian Targett
CAULKER	Philip Sully
CARPENTER	David Goodge
MADRE PACÍFICA	Jo Kendall
WOOD-CHIP LOG	Michael Graham Cox
SIRENS	Alice Arnold, Marcia King, Joan Walker
SAND-CLOCK BOY	Clive Samways
NEPTUNUS GREYBEARD	Richard Tate

SAILORS, MAGGOTS, RATS, SAILS, and other parts, were played by members of the cast.

Director: Jane Morgan

Lapping waves and, distantly, the Salve Regina, the ancient hymn sung at evening by the seaborne conquistadores. Their untrained, raucous, unaccompanied voices rise and fade on the wind.

The hymn has faded, ceased. Closer, but still a little way away, a ship's boy sings the watch:

SHIP'S BOY *(sings)*. Sand flows
                      The journey goes
                      Watches pass
                      By the glass
                      One is gone
                      The second filling
                      Turn again
                      God willing
                      Watch the sand
                      And count the glasses
                      Soon
                      The long journey passes

In the foreground, over this, we hear:

PASCAL *(close)*. Cast into the infinite immensity of spaces whereof I am ignorant and which know me not . . .

NARRATOR. Said Pascal.

PASCAL. . . . I am frightened.

The ship's boy completes his song. Then voices, close:

2ND NARRATOR. It is 1528, on the Pacific Ocean. Which has never seen a calendar; or a clock.

NARRATOR. It has a sand-clock of its own; though nothing like the Venetian kind, with its soft pink Venetian sand now passing through the waisted clock on the Ysabel —

MADRE PACÍFICA. The Ysabel. I hold her in my hand.

2ND NARRATOR. The Ysabel; whose men have no more idea of the shape of the Pacific Ocean than that Ocean has of the shape of time.

MADRE PACÍFICA (*amused*). Wasp-waisted time? Time spherical? Time sweet and bosomy. (*Teasing now; her voice fading*) Time pendulous?

NARRATOR. It is 1528; forty years before Mercator's globe unveiled the shape and confines of the earth. Then as a thing: a thing that could be shown in effigy; modelled; miniaturized; pictured —

2ND NARRATOR. Then as a thing the earth was known for the first time, and being known, was terrifying in another way: to know is no longer to *be* what you know, and to know the earth is to be something other than the earth, no longer of it but cast into an infinite immensity of spaces: in the mind.

Voices, a little way away:

NIÑO. How wind ye, Steerman?

A moment.

DE MORGA. Wind astern now — here she comes . . .

HURTADO. West, Steerman! Nothing to the north! Nothing to the south!

OMNES (*as sail is hoisted*). HOYYY! — *and the chantey begins, doggedly:*

CREW. (*Solo*) O the sun . . . (*Omnes*) I say the sun!
(*Solo*) Shining till . . . (*Omnes*) the day is done!

NIÑO. Heave on those topsail sheets now, put your backs into it!

CREW. (*Solo*) When day is done . . . (*Omnes*) we make our bed!
(*Solo*) And pray the rats . . . (*Omnes*) are too well fed!
(*Solo*) Too well fed . . . (*Omnes*) to search for meat!
(*Solo*) Too well fed . . . (*Omnes*) to gnaw our feet!

SIMÓN (*foreground, over this*). In fear and in rejoicing, weighing anchor for the last time in the New World, we embarked upon that green and spacious ocean; trusting in God, and in Don Juan Hurtado our commander. It was the Feast Day of the Invention of the Holy Cross; the air sweet-scented, full of savour, as it had been April in Seville, the sea itself smooth as the river at the Dock of Mules; a sea of polished marble broken only by the flying fish and their pursuivants...

The chantey has faded; a moment, then a sail flaps loud and sullen.

DE MORGA *(a little way away)*. Wind on the stern; but little of it.

NIÑO. Shorten sail! *(A moment; no-one moves)* Jump to it!

SIMÓN *(close)*. Yet how soon el mar pacifico, the Great Green, was turned to Mare Tenebrosum; the Green Sea of Gloom.

Voices, foreground, calm; now singly, now together: wave-like rise and fall:

CREW. *(Solo)* We, the dead
    (Omnes) Recall:
    (Singly) The air so soft that there was nothing lacking
    But the nightingale
    And the sea
    The sea smooth as a river; smooth as the Guadalquivir
    The air so full of savour that
    A dawn breeze and the wet deck drying; and the smell of the dew
    And the sea
    Smooth as a river
    Nothing lacking
    Nothing; but the nightingale
    And the sea
    The rose of morning in the sails
    White wave-caps rising from a sapphire sea
    The air as sweet and soft as April in Andalusia
    So full of savour that
    That being sailors
    Being sailors we
    Sailors
    (Omnes) We
    (Solo) Danced!

But the only sound is the occasional creaking of the 'Ysabel', becalmed.

CREW. *(Solo)* We, the drowned
    (Omnes) Recall:

YOUNG SAILOR. Days running before the gale, over white-crested water; nights under Orion, dreaming at the waistdeck; watching—see him, boys?—the Great Bear of the southern skies bathing in ocean. And the phosphorescent sea before us glittering with promises; lighting our way with fallen stars.

OLD SALT. With promises.

SHIP'S BOY. With promises.

Once more a sail flaps sullenly.

DE MORGA (*a little way away*). Wind on the stern; but little of it.

NIÑO. Watch the glass! (*A moment*) D'you hear me, boy?

SHIP'S BOY (*hastily, sings*). Watches pass
By the glass
Two are gone
The third is filling . . .

NIÑO. Man the pump there . . . (*A moment*) Jump to it!

Ship's boy completes his song, while the pump begins its horrible reluctant sucking, speeding up, then gradually slowing as the men tire.

SIMÓN (*foreground*). Eight weeks we kept our course to westward, by dead reckoning three thousand leagues and more, and made no landfall; nor shape of cloud nor flight of birds, nor scent of land to give us hope of it; no islands; nowhere to replenish food and water; while our own provisions dwindled, spawning maggots in the heat...

Background: the crew chant in time with the pump, slowing lugubriously:

CREW. Nothing to do but eat and shit
and clean the gear
and clean the ship
Nothing to do but man the pump
and clean the gear
and eat and shit
and pump
and pump
and pump . . .

SIMÓN *(foreground)*. We had suffered; so we thought; braved dangers, fear, extremes of heat and cold; known grief; endured the loss of comrades; and yet could not subdue the maggot. Puniest of creatures! and it was our undoing. The heat alone had dulled our wits, hotter than purgatorial fires; but there was worse: the rat; the cockroach; and the maggot, breeding first in that store of penguin flesh of which we had such quantity laid by; thence to the other victuals; the hardtack soon so full of weevils that many waited for darkness to eat a porridge made of it. The drinking water likewise foul and putrid now; and the rancid meat so salty it wanted a rainstorm to have satisfied our thirst; together at one gulp we could have drunk a thundercloud; but no rain came.

Pump and chant have ceased. Behind Simón a whispering has begun. Indistinct at first, then the words 'The Ysabel . . . the Ysabel . . .' *emerge, gradually becoming* 'there is a hell . . .'.

(Over this) The putrid water caused our mouths to swell, the which if any made incision of them gave forth blood as black as pitch. Our vermin fed better than we; the rats feasting upon our rotting stores; yet of all this the worst was that the maggots spawned and multiplied in all manner of cloth; and with such insolency: we ourselves could scarcely eat, while they devoured our stockings and our britches; our shirts, our smocks, our caps; till they had stripped us bare in that terrible furnace of a ship; that Ysabel once our delight, now tenanted by demons; maggot, cockroach, rat.

CREW *(whispering)*. There is a hell, the Ysabel,
　　　　　　　She's forty feet in length
　　　　　　　She's thirteen paces end to end
　　　　　　　She roams the seas with fifty men
　　　　　　　Three years at sea with fifty men
　　　　　　　And thirteen paces end to end
　　　　　　　And fifty bilge rats climbing bold
　　　　　　　Out of the slurry of the hold
　　　　　　　Out of the carcase of the ship

　　　　　　　(sickened; no longer whispered now:)

YOUNG SAILOR. 　Out of our own swill.

OLD SALT.   Maggots a-rustle in a bag; you fishermen, you've heard that filthy sound.   Our ship a cathedral to it: by night like a devoted congregation —

— the maggots hiss.   And above their hiss, recite:

MAGGOTS *(whispering)*.   Our Father
Hatch rot in Heaven
Hollow-It be Thy Name
Thy Kingdom scum
Thy Weevil dung
On Earth; rancid pees in Heaven

SAILOR.   By night the scratch and screech of rats; loathsome ministers of the abyss; ratscreech and scratch —

The rats squeak laughter; and above their squeaks, recite:

THE RATS *(whispering)*.   Devourer
Which art in Gehenna
Horror be Thy Name
Thy Carrion come
Thy Evil done
On Earth; rats at ease in Heaven

Nipped by a rat, a sailor's roaring cry; the cries spreading: 'Catch it!   Kill it!   Kill it!'; *tumult; murderous thuds, extinguishing the rat-whispers.*

Followed by one last expiring sigh:

THE RATS *(whispering)*.   Rats at ease in Heaven.

SIMÓN.   By night we longed for day, to see our tormentors; by day praying for night to cloak our blisters; we had been as naked as wild beasts, like serpents in the great heat casting off our skins, with only our corselets of mail to shield us from the sun (else put on breast and shoulder plates of armour; which none could bear); but that we took the studding sails and cut the sailcloth into tunics.   We grieved for it: when there was wind enough, and lack of sail.   And still the maggots made riot; until our sails themselves looked fed upon by locust hordes.

Voices, distantly, excited: 'Land ahead!   Land!'   'Land to starboard!'   '*Mine* the prize!' 'Two sail! Closing fast!' 'A shoal ahead!' 'Three sail!': *a cacophony of hallucinated look-out cries; rising then fading again to silence.*

No day passed but some imagined they saw land, or our vanished fleet they had forgot was burned and lost; saw fish aplenty, rushing to meet us; or the blessing of rainclouds; but they were visions, every one.

NIÑO (*a little way away*). Heave on that buntline, lads!

SIMÓN. Some days a wind came —

CREW. (*Solo, exhausted*) O the sun . . . (*Omnes, same*) I say the sun . . . (*Solo*) Shining till . . .

Silence.

SIMÓN. For ought that we could tell a gale might blow ten years on end before we found the farther shore to the Great Green; if it had one. More often we lay becalmed, our food corrupted, water foul, the sails in shreds; and soon no man that cared to keep his body covered, our skin as black as Ethiopes, whom truly we resembled: every man his lips grown huge with black and bilious blood, puffed up as if pleading for fresh water . . .

CREW (*an echoing whisper*). For water . . .

SIMÓN. . . . on that lake immense of salty ocean. Our lips puffed up as if ready to fill the sails ourselves with wind . . .

CREW (*blowing softly*). With whhhhhhhhhhhhhh . . .

SIMÓN. . . . on that great sunstruck ocean drifting . . .

The ship's bell rings; and a ship's boy sings the watch once more, in the background; now through parched and swollen lips, painfully:

SHIP'S BOY (*sings*). Sand flows
        The journey goes
        Watches pass
        By the glass
        Eight are gone
        The first is filling . . .

SIMÓN (*foreground; over this*). At noon the sun stood still. Each instant an eternity of heat. Sun above and stink below; the sailors there relieving themselves where they lay, making even the fiercest heat on deck the lesser scourge.

SHIP'S BOY (sings).   Turn again
                        God willing
                        Watch the sand
                        And count the glasses
                        Soon
                        The long journey passes . . .

NIÑO (distantly).   Heave the log, watchman!

We hear the crew begin to hum the Vexilla Regis, that hymn to crucifixion; first one man humming; the others gradually joining in; a weary trance-like humming to distract the mind from heat and thirst and pain.

SIMÓN (foreground, over the humming).   There at the mercy of the sun many grew frantic and conversed with air. Amid delectable imaginings they stepped into the sea; no man on board but saw spirits; and in a nightly tumult dreamed dreams. All things spoke to us then with tongues of angels, our ship God's universe and every thing alive with Him—

NIÑO (distantly).   Heave the log, I say!

SIMÓN.   —the sea . . .

MADRE PACÍFICA (close).   Come to me; come . . .

SIMÓN.   . . . the sails the very maggots and the wood-chip log.

MADRE PACÍFICA.   Come to my arms!

WOOD-CHIP LOG.   O, I the wood-chip log
                    Would gladly drown, my boys
                    But I haven't the strength to swim away
                    I haven't the strength to swim away
                    And you won't leave me
                    You won't leave me
                    Will you
                    Boys

THE SAILS. We the sails
        Make our last will and testament
        To the Portuguese we leave our best wind
        To the Lord the rose of morning
        To the flying fish the salt sea spray
        And our tatters
        To the maggots of the New World

THE MAGGOTS. We the maggots
        Wish to say this:
        (Close: they belch in unison, replete)

In background the humming has spread to the whole crew. In foreground:

THE CREW. We the crew
        When we had eaten all the food
        When we had eaten all the rats
        We ate
        The spiders ticks and cockroaches
        The rats' droppings
        The very maggots that so plagued us
        Lice we ate
        And then at last
        When we had eaten all the rats the cockroaches the rats'
droppings the maggots and the lice
        We dragged the sails in ocean
        Softened them
        And chewed the sailcloth
        (A moment)
        Dreaming

The humming holds a moment; ceases; then:

CREW. *(Singly)* Somo Sierra turnips!
        Illescas strawberries!
        Quinces! Quinces from Burgos . . .

OMNES *(harmoniously)*. Mmmmmmmmmmmmmm!

Distantly the shepherd's pipe and drum; dancing and faint, giddy laughter.

SIMÓN. Some that could bear the heat no longer, danced; danced madly till they fell at last into a stupor; in which fashion several of our number died.

DANCING SAILOR (*as if declaring a dying allegiance*). The zumba! Zarabanda! The chacona! The guineo! The yé-yé!

LOOK-OUT (*distant*). Land ahead! Look there, a tract of islands, boys!

OLD SALT (*close, quietly; mocking*). Mountainous; make 'em green and mountainous.

LOOK-OUT. Mountainous islands! Four of them!

OLD SALT (*as before*). Attended by crystal waterfalls; ay, and with women rushing to the shore . . .

Pipe, drum, and dancing, and the sporadic laughter, continue distantly.

THE SIRENS.   We the sirens
                Watch you go
                Come back sweet sailors of the Ysabel
                Come ride me I'm the sea
                I'm a sail catch me
                I'm a sea swallow flapping on your deck
                Stop my fall
                A flying fish gasping for breath
                Remember me

YOUNG SAILOR (*softly, hallucinating*). Look!

SIREN. Remember how we met; under the aqueduct? Have you my handkerchief still?

YOUNG SAILOR (*rising to his feet*). I remember . . .

SIREN. I'll wait for you at the Puerta del Sol.

YOUNG SAILOR. Don't go!

SIREN. Come with me then —

Others restrain the young sailor, who fights his way to the rail, past weak arms; shouts, a splash; the tumult gradually fading; over this —

SIMÓN. Some looked into the waves and saw the pastures of Gog and Magog; others a flowery plain beneath the sea; many saw islands there, garbed in the splendour of a world-desire; and jumping in, sought them in vain. Some held discourse with dead conquistadores. Some to defy the blaze of noon gazed up like the sun-staring eagle, begging the sky for rain . . .

A distant roll of thunder.

CREW. Came
    Neptunus greybeard
    Wading huge waistdeep in ocean
    Lord of disappointment
    Lord of vapour
    Watery illusion
    His trident forked with summer lightning
    His beard a morning mist
    In which he disappeared
    Laughing

Only the waves now and the creaking ship.

SIMÓN. I too was visited by creatures of my own imagining. One morning at the rising of the Dog Star came St Jerome, the founder of our order; capered a while on deck, as it seemed to me in mockery; gazing on me, as I prepared the Mass . . .

SAINT JEROME *(old, crusty, mad; but cheerful)*. When I was in the desert, dear friend, I too was fearful to look at — *(chuckling)* — as you are now; for beneath my covering my body was repulsive. Every day I gave way to tears; every day I emitted groans; ay, and with no other society than wild beasts and scorpions I imagined myself transported into the midst of virginal dances! *(Hums, amused; dances a step or two)* I was pale with fasting, and my imagination boiled with desires in a starving body; in which there raged a conflagration of the passions!

SIMÓN. How did you keep your wits, O saint our guide?

SAINT JEROME. Why by prayer of course; and the study of my imaginings; by which I learnt much.

SIMÓN. What did you learn?

SAINT JEROME. Dear friend: a riddle. The which, if you can answer it, brings peace even in the worst of torments. I will speak it in your ear. (*A moment; close, slowly:*) Why . . . is there something; instead of nothing? Eh? Why not nothing?

SIMÓN. Nothing?

SAINT JEROME (*gleeful*). Why not? Eh?

The ship's bell begins to toll, rousing the crew to prayers.

SIMÓN. And he was gone.

SHIP'S BOY (*sings*). Ocean mist
    Horizon mist
    Horizonless
    Illimitable;
    How we long for you
    You luminous
    Horizon,
    Smile of the illimitable

The bell ceases. Murmured prayers begin.

SIMÓN. Though all were sick and men died almost daily now, we never missed the Rosary, the Litanies and Te Deum at break of day, attended by the Captain-General; who afterward spoke to those most afflicted and ministered to their spirits; and once alas while he was thus from his cabin the ship's cooper, the caulker and the carpenter seized fast and bound the Slav, Don Juan's servant, took Zorya his dog and killed and ate her; then to escape a harsher death abandoned themselves to the waves.

The praying stops abruptly. Only the waves are audible.

THE COOPER, CAULKER, & CARPENTER. Ho the Ysabel
Can you still hear us?
Lads it's easier to die on a full stomach
Easier to drown
(*A moment*)

Though as I float here I still feel the old sharp wound here
in my knee

Old memories that will not die Lord so many

The field at home Lord I can smell them

Faces so clearly now

(A moment)

Can you still hear us?

Ho the Ysabel

(A moment; voices floating slowly away)

You who understand all things look down on us who
understand nothing of this our earthly burden

None of it

Nothing only this

That now Lord

Now we

Now

(A moment; faintly; one voice)

Ho the Ysabel

Silence.

SIMÓN. On the Nativity of Our Lady began our fifth month without
sight of land; now of five proud ships that set forth from the Dock of
Mules twelve months since, but one remained; of two hundred and
fifty men but thirty living, and of these barely ten were whole, or had
strength enough to hoist a sail.

*Creaks of the ship, close; waves distant now as we move below decks.
Background, Simón murmurs a prayer. In foreground, he continues:*

Among the worst infected, Alemán the astrologer, de Gálvez the
notary public, and Don Felipe our native prince returning to his
islands, lay below hatches, their sinews shrunk and black as any coal,
their skins spotted with blood of a purple colour. Despite daily
incisions the prince's veins were close to bursting open with the
pestilence; and seeing he was past hope of recovery, I prayed for his
release from pain, and from the terrible visions of his delirium.

DON FELIPE *(low)*. Do you see him, Don Melchior? Do you see him
there? Throw salt, I beg you — salt will kill him!

ALEMÁN. Alas I am too weak to fight your demons.

DON FELIPE (*close to tears*). Help me . . . have you no spells to kill him with your eyes?

ALEMÁN. Of what kind is he?

DON FELIPE. I must not speak his name. He is an asuang, one of those whose powers are acquired by eating human livers.

ALEMÁN. What powers are these?

DON FELIPE. Of sorcery. See there his black tongue. And he can fly; when he wills it, leave his lower part, grow wings, and fly. Do but cast salt on the abandoned part and he cannot reassemble himself—cast salt on him, I beg you, save me from him! (*A whisper; weeping now*) His name is wak-wak: he portends my death. Wait a little longer. O cruel to have come this far . . . and not see home again—

DE GÁLVEZ. We shall none of us see home, my friend.

ALEMÁN. Courage, de Gálvez! You and I, we shall not die till we have seen the day-star of the longed-for revelation.

DON FELIPE. What star is that, Don Melchior?

DE GÁLVEZ. He raves, man.

ALEMÁN. I tell you: it is not far off.

Distantly the bell tolls once more to call the crew to prayer. Over this—

SIMÓN. That day I too fell sick and could not rise to speak the Litanies. In dreams the saint reproached me with his eyes; and with his lips made mock of me.

SAINT JEROME (*close*). A riddle, dear friend: when is a ship not a ship? (*He giggles softly*) When Ysabel.

HURTADO (*a little way away*). Simón . . .

SIMÓN. I dreamed—or did I dream—the Captain-General brought me the book of Seth, and sat beside the saint, debating with him.

HURTADO. See how the universe bears witness to the demiurge: to the blind power that created it! Look at it now; see how it festers; peels apart like rotten fruit and shrivels in the sun . . .

SAINT JEROME. How do you keep your wits, captain our guide?

HURTADO. Why by fasting of course. See: the outward show loses its power and we are in God's hands once more; the All, Ineffable and Unbegotten One of Origin; our face to His.

SAINT JEROME *(sad, stern)*. Pray to me, Juan Hurtado, to intercede in Heaven for your soul!

HURTADO. The seeker after truth needs no such intercession, good Jerome. The light is in all men; and all Matter; all, sacred; each can find it out. And all may intercede for us; for all things are the sacrament. In all that is, runs His Blood. Hear me now; be comforted; for all things are the Bones of Christ Our Lord. And Seth, the living Christ: Seth is in all of us.

SIMÓN. My lord . . .

HURTADO. Simón?

SIMÓN *(struggles as in a dream to speak the words)*. My lord . . . why . . .

SAINT JEROME *(prompting gently)*. Instead of nothing . . .

SIMÓN. Why . . .

HURTADO. This ship? This book; this hand? Unless to some purpose; that purpose is to find out its immortal portion, stolen from the Depth by an ambitious god. This something, Simón: this hand, and yours; is an abomination, yet divine. It has the fiery spark in it; the light. This something that we are is the entanglement of Thought and Matter, spirit lost in flesh and longing to return to spirit. All things must return to the Pleroma: that region the wise call Pure Light; return to nothing and be blessed for it. Simón, the Christ took shape for this; left us His bones to show this something, Matter, when spirit has returned to aether; to show that all may intercede for us; all, sacrament; the universe itself one flesh with Christ; one dust, in Him. And if our journey fail, the world is dead matter without Thought;

and can never be redeemed.

The distant bell has ceased; a little way away, a ship's boy sings:

SHIP'S BOY *(sings).*   Ocean mist
                  Horizon mist
                  Horizonless
                  Illimitable . . .

As Simón resumes, the boy sings the same lines over, while simultaneously:

2ND SHIP'S BOY.   Sand flows
                  The journey goes
                  Watches pass
                  By the glass . . .

SIMÓN *(foreground, over this).*   That night, the last that is recorded for our voyage, Don Felipe died. At the hour of prime I joined those sound enough to climb up to the deck, in consigning his body to the waves. Our throats too swollen to utter the prayers, some lay, some knelt, others supporting themselves by the rigging . . .

Both ship's boys still singing in round or fugue, hoarsely, faltering now.

How many hours we remained so, I know not; how many hours or days; only the ship's boys still had voice, and they so tired they lost count at last, turning the clock . . .

Both boys are silent for a moment; then one uncertainly repeats his song:

2ND SHIP'S BOY.   Watches pass
                  By the glass . . .
                  (A moment; then continuing:)
                  Three are gone . . .
                  (He hesitates once more)

BERNÁLDEZ *(wearily).* Four; *four* are gone.

VOICES. Three. Three gone, watchman.

BERNÁLDEZ. Turn the glass, boy. Four are gone.

SIMÓN *(foreground).* The watchman then correcting him; the boy in tears repeating . . .

2ND SHIP'S BOY. Three, sir.

BERNÁLDEZ. *Four*, I say!

Voices rising; arguing; a weary, maddened hubbub.

SIMÓN. With voices hoarse as the chafing of an adze or the squeak of an ox-cart wheel we fell to arguing, like men touched in their honour: and for the sake of one turn of the clock dying men took each other by the throat . . .

VOICES. *Three* gone, damn your eyes! . . . by Santiago, *four!*

SIMÓN. . . . as it been our very souls at stake; yet so it seemed to us: one more turn of the clock: poor half an hour of sand: one half hour more in Hell.

Over the tumult now, a roar:

HURTADO. Enough!

Silence falls. Then the sound of glass splintering, loud and terrible.

SIMÓN. Until the Captain-General, seizing the clock, hurled it against the mast.

Out of the silence comes a sound, faint at first, as piercing as a high mouth-organ note; as it rises in volume it becomes identifiable as a human voice.

In that instant, it seemed to us, Time's chains dissolved flew about us like a salt sea spray, shrouding the light; the minutes of the day filling the air and falling to the deck sand-atomies; mere dust.

The single voice introduces an explosive choral shout: Psalm 103: 'Illic naves pertransibunt . . .'; and now a roaring sound, with a thunderous noise of waves, as of a great sea beast breaking the surface. Choir continuing: '. . . et draco iste . . .'.

Then came a noise like Heaven falling; an echo, for it was the waves erupted; and of a sudden a great sea beast surfaced at our ship's side. Whales we had seen, some in sport rubbing their backs against our keel; but this was no such play-fellow. Fully a musket-shot in length, broad-backed, its tail as big around as two hogsheads, it caused a whirlpool as it rose . . .

The choir: 'Quem formasti ad illudendum ei!'.

Though none of us had seen its like, yet we knew it for what it was: ubiquitous and immemorial, that old sea serpent, *draco iste*, lord of the abyss.

The choir ceases. In tones of thunder:

LEVIATHAN. I am the beast Leviathan; Jasconius is my name; greatest of things that swim. I am the voice out of the whirlpool, where I labour night and day to put my tail in my mouth . . . but for greatness I cannot. I am the beast Jasconius! Leviathan is my name!

SIMÓN. To these things I and others swear; on the Holy Cross. The Captain-General Don Juan Hurtado de la Vega stepped from the ship onto the serpent's back and climbed up to the head. All his beholders struck dumb; if it was a dream, all dreamed it at the same hour. Leviathan his forehead high and broad, with nostrils large, and stiff hairs standing out on either side like whiskers; his eyes like two great doors; and Juan Hurtado went in at one eye and out the other; then, coming forward, preached to us. At first we could not understand him, for he spoke in hieroglyphs as though discoursing with the angels; and his voice was the very beating and surge of the sea.

We hear Hurtado, in Leviathan's tones:

HURTADO. In the beginning was the Depth! And from it Thought arose, in Silence; begetting Spirit, which is Wisdom. And when the Depth and Silence saw this Wisdom, called Sophia, they loved her; fecundating her with the divine breath. Thus inspirited by Thought and by the Source of Light, Wisdom gave birth to perfect Christos; and to that imperfect Achamoth whom she sent to inhabit Chaos. There Achamoth, ambitious for her own domain, wove round and round; tangled herself in matter; and to it imparted life, engendering the demiurge Ildabaoth, creator of this world. We are his toy, his work; a blind god's progeny. And yet: in us the seed of Wisdom yearns still for the Source. Though we suffer through the sins of centuries; see how, mortified, the flesh yields up its song. That song is time; time and the body are one; veiling the Light eternal. You know it now; it was for this you sailed, shipmates in Christ. That Holy City pilgrims seek, it is the Source of Light; discarnate longings in the flesh, the fount and origin of pilgrimage; *fons et origo.* Sleep now, my brothers; for with you, that have encompassed all the world about, begins the promised dissolution; when all returns to Light; when we become Spirit once more, leaving this earth dull bone.

Yarilo's viol starts to play.

SIMÓN *(close).* His voice was the beating and surge of the sea; the surge of the sea.

HURTADO *(further off; slowly withdrawing).* Sleep safely in the hands of Seth your guide, immortal ancestor and heir of Adam; drink deep in dreams of the glory to come, when your standard shall be the bones of Christ, relic of relics, awaiting you where Adam, first of men, lies buried, to the east of paradise.

From the choir a huge, distant hosanna; prolonged, fading.

Then the only sound remaining is Yarilo's viol, evoking night and the threat of a sleep of death. As the viol ceases:

HURTADO *(a little way away).* Simón . . .

We hear a wind rising; the beginnings of a storm wind.

(Close; gently:) Simón. *(Then moving away; in turn:)* Bernáldez. Niño. De Morga. Méndez. *(We hear his footsteps, and his voice in the background, rousing each of the crew by name)* De la Sal. Genovés. Irés. Pero Dias . . . Pichardo . . . *(voice gradually fading)*

SIMÓN *(close).* It was night when we awoke; each man at Juan Hurtado's touch, as the Captain-General went among us. The ocean was at peace; Leviathan devoured once more of the waves; and all was still. Thin veils of cloud skimmed by the moon like the tatters of some great sail flown in shivers, while above our heads the main shrouds gusted, clutching at the wind. The pitch dark sea beneath heaved forth an oily swell.

STEERMAN *(distant, hoarse).* Wind astern . . .

Cries; calling the crew to their tasks.

SIMÓN (*close*). We stirred from sleep like men prodigiously restored; rose at the steerman's astonished cry, trimmed sails and set the watch; with one accord putting aside dissension, discontentments, sickness; even mortality itself; for though ghastly to look at, the black distemper raging in our bodies as before, yet it had not vanquished our spirits. We toiled as if Hurtado's strength and fervency of mind were now in each of us; and we his children.

Wind and waves, drowning the cries.

Long days and nights we ran before the storm, beaten this way and that by rage of weather, now fleeing the hurricane, now succumbing, pelted by rain and cataract of waves, shipping water over the bows till we scarcely knew sky from sea. At last our foremast came by the board; our yards all spent; our whipstaff broke; yet no man but withstood infirmity and took his watch on deck indifferent to peril; trusting in providence and our commander; who, ever at the steerman's side, night and day unsleeping held us steadfast to our course.

Warning shouts; barely decipherable in the storm.

We kept no record of the hours; nor the days; no Mass was said, no Salve sung; prayers we murmured for God's ears alone, in words soon swallowed by the wind. What day it was; what night rather, for it was near the hour of Compline; when we first sighted land, I can but guess at. Near enough, St Matthew's eve; the saint forgive me; we had shed the ways of Christian men, after five months at sea in mien and in attire ruder than galley slaves, and more like savages than those upon whose mercy we were then cast up; as if disgorged of Neptune.

More shouts as men battle to shorten sail.

Powerless to resist the winds, we saw ourselves driven in among banks and rocks, and there buffeted, like to founder; hurled onto a lee shore; had we not stuck fast. We fled the ship, which by God's mercy dragged ashore unharmed, coming to rest on her beam ends; where once we were come safe to land ourselves, we made her fast, and sought out shelter where we could.

The sounds of storm and shipwreck slowly fade to silence.

A tinkling of bells, close. A moment's stillness; outdoor stillness without distant wind or wave; distantly, birdsong. Then the rising murmurs of the Sultan's court. The bells jangle once more; gongs are struck, and the murmurs slowly cease.

Some way off, a voice, melodious, commanding; in a language utterly strange.

SULTAN. *Cansun rahia! Cansun bassal rahia, bassal tihan!* [Welcome, lord; welcome, great one] *(A moment) Marica, marica! Marica, tihan.* [Approach . . .]

BERNÁLDEZ *(nearer).* My lord . . .

HURTADO. Stay close, Bernáldez.

SULTAN. *Marica!*

ALEMÁN. He bids you approach.

HURTADO. Be bold of friendship, but do him no homage; come.

Court murmurs rise once more as they advance.

SIMÓN *(close).* When we had gained sufficient strength to explore the neighbouring regions, we were brought into the presence of the *rahia*, the King or Sultan of that place, an island large and pleasant called in their language Seram; the islanders comely and as tall as we, their hair exceedingly black and falling to their shoulders. Some wore silk; their nobles gold earrings; all were perfumed; and they made show of all love and familiarity, reverencing the Captain-General according to the custom of that country.

A wave of approving sound from the bystanders as Hurtado greets his hosts.

HURTADO. In the name of King Charles of Spain our lord and Emperor; and that of his Redeemer and ours, Christ our Saviour; we bring you greetings.

SULTAN *(admiring Hurtado's stature and his beard).* *Pixao! (Murmurs of agreement from the court) Mahin guay! Mahin bonghot! (Offering cushions) Uliman? Minuncubil, rahia? (A moment) Minuncubil?*

ALEMÁN. *Minuncubil* . . . before good Don Felipe died he spoke this often. The Sultan asks if we would drink.

HURTADO (to the Sultan) We will drink with you, sir.

SULTAN (calls). Bonsul: palatin comorica bassal tagha . . .

Court murmurs rise once more; in foreground:

SIMÓN (close). In his palace we were served turtle eggs in porcelain dishes; beside them jars of palm wine from which we drank in their fashion, through small reeds; and for our sickness a draught called by them tubin molanghai; which was, they said, a great poison but made harmless by infusion of certain of their medicinable herbs.

To the court's amusement, the Sultan tries to break down the language barrier:

SULTAN. Siama siama, rahia. [All is the same.] Guay . . .

ALEMÁN. Face.

SULTAN. Guay, mahin guay. Guay.

ALEMÁN. Guay.

SULTAN. Guay. Matta. Matta.

ALEMÁN. Eyes. Matta.

SULTAN. Delengan . . . ilon . . .

ALEMÁN. Ears. Nose.

SULTAN. Olol . . .

ALEMÁN. Lips. Olol.

SULTAN. Dilla. (Sticking out his tongue) Dilla!

ALEMÁN. Tongue. (Doing likewise). Dilla . . .

SULTAN (delighted). Dilla! Siama siama!

THE COURT. Siama siama!

HURTADO. Tongue.

SULTAN (tentatively) Tongue . . .

HURTADO. Tongue . . .

As the court picks up and tries out the word 'tongue', the sounds fade, intersecting with a new, rising acoustic, reed pipes playing in the distance: nearer, a girl instructs her lover, reciting . . . usa, dua, tolo, — [one, two, three] —upat, lima, onom, pito, guala, siam, polo . . .

We hear, amid giggles, Alemán's first steps in the Tagalog language.

SIMÓN *(foreground, over this).* The first to gain some mastery of their language was Melchior Alemán, and he soon learned the whereabouts of those Moluccas or Maluchoes and other isles of spice on which, by the King's edict, we were not to set foot. Taking the sun in 13°10′, the Captain-General ascertained that we were already within the line granted to John of Portugal; yet since the islanders knew nothing of our treaties made in Europe, and since we had landed there by God's will and no design of our own, we told them nothing; rather assuring them of our protection now and henceforward, our men being eager to refit the ship at their ease, and gather such treasure in spices and precious metals as could be attributed to trade or plunder got within the Spanish line; which was done without the knowledge of our Captain. All his care was to discover the realm of Prester John, that Christian King in whose keeping might be found that great relic he sought.

The Tagalog lesson has faded. Once more wind and waves, distantly. And a many-throated native chant.

To this end the Sultan of Seram furnished us with a bark, lateen-rigged as the Moorish vessels are, and swift; and men to sail her. Besides the Captain-General came Yarilo his servant, I myself, Bernáldez the marshal, Alemán now our interpreter, and Peralonso Méndez, like Bernáldez an old comrade-in-arms of Juan Hurtado, and faithful always; in Seram we left to guard and restore the Ysabel, her master Niño, the pilot de Morga, and the crew; with Tomás de Gálvez, the notary public, to stay by the Sultan as emissary to his court; for he was glad to be done with the sea a while. Three months and more we sailed from island to island, some hospitable, others warlike, but all in mortal awe of those our weapons, muskets, falconets, and culverins, brought with us from our ship. Yet none could tell us ought of

Christian kings, or Christian bones. Presbyter John, some said, was slain long since by the Great Khan of China. There were no Christians, they adjured us to believe them, east of paradise; nor secret temples; nor yet relics of antiquity; save one . . .

The chant has faded; nearer now a voluble Moluccan crowd, and a sailor from Seram translating for Alemán:

SAILOR. *Lac bassal tihan! Bassal paha, bassal camat. Abba tihan!*

OTHER VOICES (*concurring*). *Bassal abba lac . . . bassal tihan, rahia!*

ALEMÁN. My lord — they speak of the bones of one who lived in ancient times! And dwelt here on an island . . .

SAILOR (*amid other voices*). *Candingar . . . mahin candin!*

ALEMÁN (*translating as they talk*). The isle of goats . . . he dwells atop a mountain; one in stature like a god . . .

A moment; native voices still talking.

HURTADO (*close*). Now great Seth be praised. Where is this island?

The crowd sounds fade. A drumbeat, distant at first, begins; as it draws nearer, other sounds are heard accompanying it: axe and machete blows in undergrowth.

SIMÓN. Thus it was we came at last to Candigar, where this tale is written and this true relation made; that isle where presently we dwell marooned; now and forever; Yarilo who never speaks; Alemán who speaks to the stars, even by day; old Bernáldez, sick at heart; Méndez the cheerful; and I. An isle some twenty miles long; not above six broad; our empire; nay our universe, our all. O how fine we thought it, that first day we saw it with its clouded peak, its verdure in such abundance, and the paraquetoes that flew like lesser clouds of red and green along the valleys where we marched; marched and climbed, to Yarilo's drum; climbed and hacked our way, thinking at every step: we six! we six of all the world the first since Golgotha to look upon the Christ!

The machete sounds have ceased. The drumbeats end in a flourish.

We hear the mountaintop wind. Very distantly a bleating goat. A pause.

At last one sob of horror: Hurtado's.

SERAM SAILOR. *Lac abba tihan, rahia* . . .

A moment.

HURTADO. What manner of place is this?

Distantly: mocking cries of parakeets.

SIMÓN (*close*). Bones there were; aplenty; on our cloudy mountain top; it was a place of skulls indeed, but not of Christian burial; the wind their only winding-sheet. All wept; even our captain.

HURTADO (*through tears*). Friends, was it of these they spoke?

SIMÓN (*close*). Bones unburied, scattered on the ground; dragged there perhaps; yet to what purpose? Our islanders could not say; here they had lain in horrid profusion since their forefathers found them: the bones of men who had climbed to this summit, here to die? How often Alemán and I have pondered this; the bones of seafarers shipwrecked before us, gathered on this vantage point to seek in vain a glimpse of sail? Or merely the bones of other men punished as we, confined to this place, *candin-gar*, the place of goats? Men of great stature they were not; they were but men, though some notable by the seeming hugeness of their skulls. Sometimes I think of them as our own; our bones, in a vision foreseen; for when we die at last, we shall join them there to lie bleached and forgotten in the sun.

We hear the wind a moment; the distantly bleating goat. Fade to silence.

The sound of the Seram bells, close. And a man mumbling brokenly to himself, over a book:

HURTADO (*under his breath*). . . . discarnate longings in the flesh; chapter four, verse thirteen, the first tractate of Seth . . . (*turning pages*) I am the first and last; the honoured and the scorned; I am the whore, and the Holy One . . .

BERNÁLDEZ (*a little way away*). Don Juan.

HURTADO. Discarnate longings. Here . . . I am knowledge; and ignorance; I am shameless; and ashamed; I am strength, and I am fear—

BERNÁLDEZ. My lord, Tomás de Gálvez would speak with you. *(A moment)* My lord?

HURTADO *(as before, still mumbling)*. I am foolish, and I am wise. I am godless, and I am one whose God is great. Here endeth Thunder, Perfect Mind.

Crying now, Hurtado closes the book.

SIMÓN *(close)*. From Candigar we returned together to Seram, heavy-hearted; the Captain-General broken in spirit. Seeing him distracted, we wept anew; for we were fatherless.

DE GÁLVEZ. Captain. Don Juan: it is I, Tomás de Gálvez.

HURTADO *(more clearly)*. I am the Voice. I move in every creature. I am the Invisible One within the All.

DE GÁLVEZ. Good sir: we must put to sea. There is an armada come to the Maluchoes, they say from Portugal. Four sail; some say more; two hundred men, with fifty cannon. Good my lord, if we remain we are but thirty men against a mighty fleet. The Ysabel is ready, well provisioned, and the crew assembled; with your consent I—

HURTADO *(interrupting)*. Know you how it was Wisdom conceived herself? Good friend, it was upon this fashion: from the nine Muses, one separated away; she came to a high mountaintop—mark you—and spent time seated there, so that she desired herself alone . . . *(secretively low)* . . . in order to become androgynous. She fulfilled her desire. Ay, and became pregnant from it!

He chuckles quietly. Fading, then—

Rising sounds of revelry; music; a hubbub in several tongues. Farther off, the Sultan is delivering an oration in Tagalog; his words drowned by talk.

SIMÓN *(close)* On the eve of our departure the Sultan gave a banquet; all present exchanging vows and promises of perdurable friendship, the which we knew could never be maintained; and only ate and drank the more . . .

HURTADO. Alemán.

ALEMÁN *(hubbub continuing around them).* My lord?

HURTADO. Make known to the Sultan that I am *not* of those who flee his kingdom.

ALEMÁN. Not, sir?

HURTADO. I must stay; to build a shrine.

ALEMÁN. No, captain.

HURTADO. I tell you I shall. Alemán: will you not help me build it?

ALEMÁN *(a moment).* Here on Seram?

HURTADO. On Candigar. Come, say you will.

ALEMÁN *(delaying, overcome with pity).* To whom will it be raised?

HURTADO. Why, to Our Saviour and those His apostles whose bones we lately saw there, you and I.

ALEMÁN. How can that be, my lord?

HURTADO. Not those heretics who falsely called him Lord; not they Alemán; these are His true disciples followed Him into the grave, their bones rescued by the Arimathean and hidden in the caves where lived Mesopotamian Nestor; one such was Mary Magdalen. Did you not see a woman's bones there on our sacred mountain?

ALEMÁN. I . . . I cannot say. Don Juan—

HURTADO *(his mood turning).* You took an oath with me. Have you forgotten it? *(A moment, then getting to his feet; voice rising, gradually hushing the assembly)* Have you all forgotten? The cord; the water; and the fire? *(A moment; raging; tearful)* You are traitors; all; for by Ouraios and Astaphaios: Seth is dead in you! All dead men that would leave this holy place! You that were purified, and baptized at my hand: I curse you now, children of base Ildabaoth! *(Weeping)* All dead!

Silence has fallen; gradually murmurs rising, as the acoustic fades.

Cannon firing, some way off, in a dull, steady, salute, as the Ysabel weighs anchor. Distantly, wind and waves.

SIMÓN *(foreground).* It was a ghostly ship that sailed next day, for those aboard had fallen sick; and that grievously. After the feasting we lay stricken with cramps; as we thought then indicted by our own excesses; but these alas were not the cause of it. We who had been with him to Candigar could not abandon Juan Hurtado; and he would not leave; though he of all our company alone was free of that strange sickness which afflicted us.

Cannon still firing, dully, rhythmically; growing distant.

SIMÓN. Niño the master, de Morga, and de Gálvez now their captain led the crew to the Ysabel, though some so faint they barely crawled aboard.

CREW *(close, murmuring).* Pray for us!

NIÑO *(close, weak).* Farewell, Fray Simón; do but convert these islanders to the true faith, and you need not fear the Portuguese; God will protect His servant. I pray He restore Hurtado's senses; assuredly the Emperor will send a fleet for him. *(A moment)* Farewell.

DE MORGA *(weaker still).* I beg you, pray for us!

CREW *(murmurs; fading).* Now and at the hour of our death.

DE GÁLVEZ *(distant).* Pray for us!

The last cannon fires, distant now; only the waves remain, fading to silence.

Rising, the sound of Yarilo's viol, played roughly, bitterly; discordant.

SIMÓN. We watched their sails into the distance; heard their cannon fade. At the hour of Prime I made my way to Juan Hurtado's chamber, there to say a Mass for all our souls; those ashore and those departed. There I found Yarilo playing and weeping; on my enquiring of the Captain-General he only shook his head.

The viol breaks off with jarring abruptness.

Then laying his viol aside, he drew from the Captain-General's possessions the leathern cask; unlocked it; and brought forth a jar of liquid, which he gave me, motioning me to open it. I knew it by its smell: it was *tubin molanghai*, that poison we had partaken of, on our arrival; then made medicinable by those herbs they brewed in it; yet this vial contained no herbs. At first I feared for our commander's life; but by Yarilo's face I knew my fears were needless; and I understood why the Slav wept. The Captain-General had poisoned us, every one.

After a moment, bells, and the palace gongs summoning the court. Distantly, a tirade in Tagalog: the Sultan, raging.

Those aboard the Ysabel no man could save; and though our own physic was close at hand, growing plentifully upon the island, there was no serviceable herb could shield us from the Sultan's wrath. For he received embassage from the Portuguese, who told him of those their treaties with the Emperor; how ours were lies, and void; how we had deceived him. His rage as great now as once his kindness, he pledged to avenge himself on the Captain-General. Yet at our entreaties, and for his former love to us, seeing how we had suffered at our captain's hands, he did not betray us to our enemies.

The Sultan's harangue fades. A sound of running footsteps; indoor acoustic:

ALEMÁN (*stops a little way away; out of breath*). Where is the fiend Hurtado?

A moment.

MÉNDEZ (*nearer; quietly*). You do him wrong; the fiend torments him no longer.

ALEMÁN. Is he dead?

BERNÁLDEZ. Look in your star-books, Alemán: his fate is crueller than death. He walks the shore, tears at his clothes and flesh, calling down pity from the skies that have too late restored his wits.

ALEMÁN. His life is forfeit. (*A moment*) His for ours. So the Sultan decrees it.

A silence.

MÉNDEZ. Better to die with him.

ALEMÁN. Better to live than die *for* him: if it be true he sought to kill us.

MÉNDEZ. I say this cannot be his work.

ALEMÁN. I say it is.

A moment.

BERNÁLDEZ. Fray Simón, you are his chaplain still. If he make confession of it . . .

ALEMÁN. Ay, what then? *(A moment)* Will you still die for him, Bernáldez?

A moment.

BERNÁLDEZ. I cannot kill him.

ALEMÁN. Méndez?

MÉNDEZ. He has the strength of ten; and we are sick.

ALEMÁN. Of poison, friends. Poison robs the strongest of their powers, and in sufficient quantity will it not kill great Seth himself?

No-one answers. Silence.

A chill sound of bells. Then:

HURTADO *(close).* Simón . . .

A moment.

Do you believe in the resurrection of the flesh?

A moment.

It shall be at the last judgement, Simón; and only then. I have sinned greatly; in word and deed; denied the one true God; worshipped false teachings; and murdered in their name. Humbly I kneel before this bread; this wine; I that forsook His body for a demon bred of Moorish books. As you are Christ's true minister still, from all false vows released, grant me forgiveness of these my sins. This flesh. *(He takes the sacramental bread; a moment)* This blood. *(He drinks)* They are the only sacrament; the one path to the living Christ. *(A moment)*

Will you not bless me?

SIMÓN *(blessing him; barely able to speak the words:)*. In the name of God the Father, God the Son, and God the Holy Ghost, Amen.

HURTADO. Praise be to God Almighty; in whose name I yield to Mother Church.

SIMÓN *(softly)*. Laus Deo.

A moment.

HURTADO. My spirit faints . . . help me to these cushions. *(A moment)* Bring me my books.

Simón fetches them.

I fought for her glory once; fought to defend our Church. Did you ever hear tell of it?

SIMÓN. I did, my lord.

HURTADO *(proudly)*. 'In May the Janissaries marched
    Against Bohemia. Louis of Hungary
    Was trembling as I stood before him,
    Bearing orders from the Emperor!
    We left Shabotz to Suleiman
    On the Eighth of July—
    But we disputed Belgrade! As
    The world knows, and Suleiman!
    Suleiman, Selim's son,
    The lesser soldier but the greater man:
    He kept his word at Rhodes, by Seth!
    When the Grandmaster sued for peace . . .'

He wavers; in pain now, but continuing:

        'I fought this warrior
        And poet, Lord of Lords
        In the Carpathians,
        Vlad the Impaler at my side
        And Young Szapolyi The Effeminate
        And the Ban of Banát. We were taken at last

> At Mitrovitz . . .'

Breaking off; breathing with difficulty:

We danced the zumba, he and I; Suleiman; in the courtyard there, beneath the pines. At Mitrovitz, that sea-cold fortress.

SULEIMAN *(an echo; close, caressingly).* Don Juan. Don Juan Hurtado de la Vega. Don Juanito.

HURTADO *(flinging down the books).* Burn them all, these Moorish lies. I had them . . . *(breaking off again; a spasm)* . . . from his hand. You have poisoned me, Simón; I know it. I feel it in my veins: *tubin molanghai.* How?

SIMÓN *(close).* I could not speak.

A moment.

HURTADO. O child. In the communion wine? Then you are damned eternally. I thank you for it, boy; one friend the more in Hell.

Fighting off his death spasms; fierce:

> 'While I, with a handful of arquebusiers
> Was salting Barbarossa's tail,
> Till Suleiman himself came forth
> One April morning from Constantinople,
> Eighty thousand strong. Louis of Hungary
> Was slow, that weak Bohemian.
> Who else but Vlad the Devil,
> And the Ban, and I,
> Braved the Ottoman at Mohacs, on the plain!
> The Transylvanians advanced, we met them
> With a cannonade and charged
> The first line with the heavy cavalry.
> We *broke* the feudal serfs! Too well —
> Our guns were slow to follow.
> When the Janissaries struck us
> From the right, we drove them off
> And smashed the second line — but
> The artillery! They chained their cannon

Together, by the grey Danube.
We could not pierce their cannon,
On the plain of Mohacs. By . . . Santiago . . .

With a last effort; a cry:

Seven Bishops died that day!'

He dies; and the indoor acoustic fades.

Slowly replaced by the Candigar acoustic; distant waves; wind, bird cries.

We hear Simón's voice, some way off:

SIMÓN *(sings)*. Give thanks
To the light of day
To Him that sends
The night away
And Her to Whom
All sailors pray
Bless the cross
Glorious tree
And the Lord
Of Veritie
And the Holy
Trinitie
Bless the soul
Given to all
That sons of Eve
After the Fall
May their immortal
Portion call
Give thanks!

Over the song we hear, closer, in an echo acoustic:

HURTADO. Your name, boy?

SIMÓN. Simón Pérez, Captain.

HURTADO. Age?

SIMÓN. Sixteen, captain.

HURTADO. Ever held mass on a swaying deck with the salt spray in your eyes?

SIMÓN. No, sir.

HURTADO. Have you learnt any songs fit for a sailor's ears, Simón?

SIMÓN. Yes.

HURTADO. Then sing one . . .

The song comes to an end. The wind and distant waves audible. Far off, a bleating goat.

SIMÓN *(foreground)*. We buried him on Candigar, the place of goats, beside the bones that were his hope and his despair; a place no longer terrible to us; familiar now; a place of reconciliation. Yet in truth: our lives were ended at the hour of his death. The Sultan brought us here for our better protection; saying, so Alemán reports, that we might yet be rescued if we still had our Emperor's love. Yet what is the love of an Emperor? When the love of Him who saved us is denied. I mean our Lord; for I believe we die in Juan Hurtado's love. Until that day we live like Christians; yet like savages; like sailors, for we watch the sea, and sing the Salve joyously at evening.

In the background we hear Yarilo strike up a tune.

Yarilo has his viol; he plays the zumba, zarabanda, the chacona, the guineo, the yé-yé . . .

A moment.

And being sailors . . . . we dance.

The viol continues, until a choral hymn, rising slowly, vies with it, then drowns it:

The Salve Regina, the ancient hymn sung every evening by the seaborne conquistadores. Their untrained, raucous, unaccompanied voices swell and fade on the wind.

CAREY HARRISON is a novelist and playwright whose plays for Radio 3 include the highly praised *A Suffolk Trilogy* (also available from Oleander Press), beginning with *I Never Killed My German*, winner of the Giles Cooper Award for Best Play of 1979. Born in 1944 to actor parents Sir Rex Harrison and Lilli Palmer, Carey Harrison turned to playwriting on leaving Cambridge, and his performed work comprises a dozen stage plays and over 90 TV scripts including the BBC-2 drama series *Freud*. A quartet of novels entitled *To Liskeard*, and starting with *Richard's Feet*, begins publication from Heinemann in March 1990, concurrently with *From The Lion Rock* and *The Sea Voyage*.

OLEANDER DRAMASCRIPTS

ARISTOTLE'S MOTHER: a Radio Play
Sir Herbert Read

GARRITY & OTHER PLAYS for Stage and Radio
Philip Ward

LORD BYRON AT THE OPERA: a Radio Play
Sir Herbert Read

TELEVISION PLAYS
Philip Ward

A SUFFOLK TRILOGY: Radio Plays
Carey Harrison

OLEANDER LANGUAGE AND LITERATURE

FRENCH KEY WORDS
Xavier-Yves Escande

A LIFETIME'S READING
Philip Ward

CELTIC: A Comparative Study
D. B. Gregor

MARVELL'S ALLEGORICAL POETRY
Bruce King

ROMONTSCH: Language and Literature
D. B. Gregor

INDONESIAN TRADITIONAL POETRY
Philip Ward

ROMAGNOL: Language and Literature
D. B. Gregor

THE ART & POETRY OF C.-F. RAMUZ
David Bevan

FRIULAN: Language and Literature
D. B. Gregor

GREGUERIAS: Wit and Wisdom
Ramón Gómez de la Serna